Finding F

Finding Faith

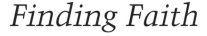

THE SPIRITUAL QUEST OF THE POST-BOOMER GENERATION

RICHARD FLORY AND
DONALD E. MILLER

RUTGERS UNIVERSITY PRESS
New Brunswick, New Jersey, and London

LIBRARY OF CONGRESS CATALOGING-IN-PUBLICATION DATA

Flory, Richard W.
   Finding faith : the spiritual quest of the post-boomer generation /
Richard Flory and Donald E. Miller.
      p.   cm.
   Includes bibliographical references (p.) and index.
   ISBN 978-0-8135-4272-0 (hardcover : alk. paper)—ISBN 978-0-
8135-4273-7 (pbk. : alk. paper)
   1. Generation X—Religious life.   I. Miller, Donald E. (Donald
Earl), 1946– II. Title.
   BV4529.2.F57   2008
   306.60973—dc22   2007022102

A British Cataloging-in-Publication record for this book is available
from the British Library.

Copyright © 2008 by Richard Flory and Donald E. Miller

Visit our Web site: http://rutgerspress.rutgers.edu

Manufactured in the United States of America

CONTENTS

PREFACE

THIS BOOK BEGAN LIFE SEVERAL YEARS AGO in a conversation we had about a potential follow-up project to our *GenX Religion* book, based on our observations of many young Christians we knew who were giving up on the relatively sterile, rationalist Protestant worship they were experiencing in their churches. In this, we saw them making what to us was a fairly radical switch from, say, a Presbyterian church or a Baptist church to a Catholic, Episcopal, or Orthodox church for, among other reasons, the full-bodied experience of a worship service in one of these traditions. The radical thing to us was that they could make that switch given the different conceptions of theology, including such strange—at least to Protestants—practices as venerating the saints, praying to Mary, or kissing the garments of the priest. When we started asking questions of these young adults, we found that they were much more interested in what we have come to call the "embodied spirituality" inherent in these traditions, where, as one person told us, participating in the different elements of the liturgy is like "being in the orchestra instead of watching a performance."

We initially conceived of the project as "the recovery of ritual," where we saw the central piece of what we were trying to figure out being the attraction of the embodied and ritualistic aspects of these traditions. However, as we started visiting different churches and interviewing different Post-Boomers, we quickly discovered that there was much more going on than just a "recovery of ritual" in ancient Christian traditions. There was also the invention, importation, and adaptation of ritualistic elements into churches that had never included such elements in their worship services before, and a new emphasis on living out, or embodying, their faith commitments back into the larger community and not being content to simply stay within their religious communities pursuing an individualistic spiritual quest. As well, we found a backlash movement that has organized to counter these different types of developments within Christianity, which in itself let us know that we were really on to something, in that if a reactionary movement of sorts—a term that one of their number proudly uses to describe their efforts— had already organized against what we were barely becoming aware of, there must be something significant developing.

We now believe that we are witnessing another potential revolution in how Christians worship and associate with each other. While the masses are still lining up to enter mega churches that are distinguished by boring architecture, casually dressed clergy, and pop Christian music, the "Post-Boomer" generation—those young people ranging in age from their twenties to their forties—is having second thoughts. Increasingly, they want a worship space that is aesthetically rich, participative, and relatively intimate—a place where one can actually experience community rather than be entertained. A lot has happened in the last decade since commentators such as Donald Miller (1997) started noticing a new style of Christianity being birthed in the United States. Now almost everyone has access to the Internet, no one younger than thirty buys a camera that uses film, and music is stored on tiny wafers that hold thousands of songs. But another thing occurred. This generation grew up with parents who were seldom home. These kids had to raise themselves, and often in chaotic circumstances. Today they don't want to be stimulated so much as loved. Living without structure is pretty empty after a while, which is prompting at least a few members of this generation to experiment with a new take on God, the appropriation of tradition, and beliefs that are preceded by practice—yes ritual—which, of course, their parents thought was only for premodern cultural illiterates. This postmodern generation is not coming to religion by way of rational proofs and argumentation. They are spiritual beings who are seeking aesthetically rich experiential forms to give definition to their lives.

This book is actually the last installment of several different pieces of this project that we have made public. Of course, we have followed the traditional academic path in some of what we have done by making conference presentations and publishing articles or chapters based on our findings. But less traditionally, at least for sociologists, we produced an art gallery installation that showed in three different galleries in southern California from 2003 to 2004. These installations were actually the first public presentations of our findings and caused no small amount of concern in certain segments of Christianity, including the evangelical magazine *Christianity Today* (Olson 2003), yet our experience in mounting those exhibitions was invaluable, both in terms of what we learned about how people interacted with visual information and for what it told us about the people we were actually studying. Suffice it to say, some people were very happy with what we included in the shows, while others suggested that we represented everything from the worst examples of postmodernism to people who were actively promoting an anti-Christian and anti-religious perspective. Indeed, one right-wing pundit, basing his response on a *Los Angeles Times* article on our installation, said that we were prime evidence of the "anti-God" bias among university professors (Shapiro 2004, 87–88). An interesting observation, to be sure, but one that neither of us would claim to be true regarding our own views. Of course, it might have helped that writer to have actually seen the show—which we discovered was the common denominator among those who didn't like what they thought we were doing.

They hadn't actually set foot into any of the three galleries in which we mounted the installation.

In the end, all of the experiences we have had with this project have served to make this a better book, even the one involving our supposed anti-God bias! We are grateful to the many people who have participated with us in this project, from conference participants to the many visitors to the galleries where the installation was on display, particularly those who engaged us in conversation about our project and in the process contributed more than they know to our understanding of Post-Boomer religion. As well we are grateful to the many individuals, congregations, and ministries that allowed us to spend time with them, to interview them, and to simply get to know them and to understand their motivations in the particular ways that they approach their faith commitments.

We are particularly indebted to the Louisville Institute for their support of this project, to the Alban Institute (www.alban.org) for permission to use material previously published in our article "Expressive Communalism" (*Congregations* 30, no. 4 [fall 2004]: 31–35), and to Ashgate Publishers (www.ashgate.com) for permission to use material from "The Embodied Spirituality of the Post-Boomer Generations," published in *A Sociology of Spirituality*, edited by Kieran Flanagan and Peter C. Jupp (Aldershot, Hampshire, UK: Ashgate, 2007).

We would also like to specifically mention a particularly important collaboration that we developed as a part of this project with Dan Callis (www.callisart.com), an artist and friend who was invaluable in his contributions to this project, particularly as it relates to the gallery installations and photography, but also in the way that he saw and understood the developments we were trying to understand from the perspective of an artist. Not only were the installations full collaborations with Dan, and would not have taken place without his expertise, but his observations through that process and throughout the project improved the final outcome as seen in this book.

Finally, we, as it seems everyone does who writes a book such as this, would like to say that our conclusions are in fact our own, and sometimes are at variance with what others suggested that we should do. We are certain as well that, just as with our experiences with the gallery installations, there are those who won't like where we may have placed them in our typology or even for subjecting their religious activities to academic study. As such, we are happy to own up to the successes and failures of our arguments in this book. As we suggested in the gallery installations, we are vitally interested in starting a conversation about what the developments we have observed may mean not only for Christianity, but perhaps also for other religious traditions. We include only Christian groups in our analysis here, but we suspect that similar developments are taking place within Judaism and Islam, particularly as these traditions seek to both engage their young adults and to keep them interested and involved in their congregations. We look forward to others taking our results and seeing if they have any applicability in these other traditions.

Finding Faith

CHAPTER 1

Introduction

RELIGION, IT SEEMS, is everywhere in the news. Whether abroad in various war zones like Afghanistan or Iraq or in persistent crisis situations such as between the Israelis and Palestinians, religion plays a central organizing role in the events taking place there. At home, religion plays a role in seemingly everything from presidential elections to immigration (we're now seeing T-shirts and bumper stickers that ask, "Who would Jesus deport?"), to such issues as gay marriage, abortion, and the teaching of intelligent design as science in public schools. America, most polls show, is one of the most religious nations in the world, with upward of 90 percent of the population claiming to believe in God, and anywhere from about 20 to 40 percent of the population, depending on the poll and its methodology, claiming to regularly attend religious services. Further, religion in America has undergone a public revival of sorts since the 1980s, from the rise of the Moral Majority and the religious right to more recent efforts at federal funding for faith-based social welfare programs. This suggests that religion has taken a much more pronounced role in the everyday life of American society that is likely more extensive than most people realize, and perhaps a greater role than many people would desire.

However, despite the role that religion plays in the personal lives of individual Americans and increasingly in the public sphere, there continues to be both a lack of understanding about the importance of religion and a lack of knowledge about the particular beliefs of different religious groups, and how these may motivate their actions in culture and society. Boston University religious studies professor Stephen Prothero has recently written a best-selling book about the average American citizen's stunning lack of knowledge about religion in general, and even about basic tenets of their own religious faith (2007). Prothero frames this as both a domestic civic problem and as a problem for international relations. As a domestic problem, he argues, it is virtually impossible to understand much of American history without understanding the role of religion and the particular beliefs that motivated such historic movements as abolitionism, women's rights, and civil rights. He argues further that in order to participate as a knowledgeable citizen in current debates about, for example, abortion, family values, intelligent design, and the like, it is necessary to understand the religious perspectives of those on each side of these issues. As a problem for international relations, he argues that we are doomed to misunderstand major international conflicts unless we understand the ancient differences between, for example, Islam, Judaism, and Christianity. University of Southern California religion and media scholar and journalist Diane Winston has similarly pointed out that in the press, reporters often miss the significant role that religion plays in a particular story that may seem otherwise unrelated to religion. Winston argues that this isn't necessarily because journalists are hostile or suspicious toward religion, but that they fail to really understand how important religion is in the various stories they pursue. Winston argues that journalists "need to 'get' religion; not just its sociopolitical significance but also its ideas and beliefs—if they want to faithfully cover today's world" (2004; see also Beckerman 2004 for a similar argument).

On the other hand, other recent best-selling books that are much more hostile to religion have essentially called for a less tolerant view toward religion, at least in public life, and suggest that if religion were eradicated, the world would be a much better place as a result. Oxford University evolutionary biologist Richard Dawkins, in a book with the less-than-subtle title *The God Delusion* (2006), has argued that the belief in God is essentially a "misfiring" of human mental processes that has no survival value in the evolutionary process. It is essentially a genetic—or his term, memetic—mistake, albeit for Dawkins a particularly costly one, in that in his view any good that religion has done throughout history is far outweighed by the evil and violence it has sponsored and motivated. Similarly, Sam Harris (2005; 2006) has written two recent books in which he suggests that if religion were subjected to modern rational and scientific standards, it would lose power and eventually cease to exist, because it is an irrational, primitive holdover that modern societies have simply tolerated, much to their detriment. Harris was initially motivated by the events of 9/11, and ultimately concludes, with Dawkins, that the world would be much better off without the influence of religion, as it has motivated far more evil than good in the world.

Our approach would be more in tune with Prothero and Winston rather than Dawkins or Harris, since despite what Dawkins and Harris argue, and regardless of whether they are right or wrong about the ultimate truth of religion, the point is that religion isn't going anywhere anytime soon. As such, both individuals and nations must come to at least a basic understanding of different religious perspectives and how these motivate the actions of their adherents, since religion continues to be one of the most fundamental organizing schemas that individuals and groups have for their lives and their actions in the world. As Prothero has put it, "religion is the most volatile constituent of culture, because religion has been, in addition to one of the greatest forces for good in world history, one of the greatest forces for evil" (2007, 4). While this book is not about how different religious groups and individuals may order their actions toward any particular public or political issue, it is about how different groups interact with, understand, and frame the relationship between the larger culture and their religious beliefs. We would suggest that if we can understand how groups such as we present here approach religion, it may provide a window onto other issues in terms of how and why they act in particular ways in a variety of different societal spheres, such as culture, politics, and morals, whether personal or social.

As important as it is to understand religion in the context of national issues and international relations, particularly in an increasingly globalizing world in which one's neighbor can as easily be Muslim or Hindu as Jewish or Christian, it is also important to understand how particular religious communities and traditions are currently responding to various cultural challenges and opportunities that they identify as confronting them. Although this book is framed around issues of Post-Boomer religious beliefs and, in particular, focuses on Christian groups, we believe that it is also helpful to think of the approaches/perspectives presented here as places where new and emerging forms of religious expression will start and then filter into entire religious institutions and belief systems. That is, all religions need to both maintain the faith of their young people and keep them in the fold, as it were, in order to remain viable—they can't survive on converts alone. Indeed, recent research suggests that the twenties-to-forties age range is particularly problematic for all religious faiths in terms of attracting and maintaining young believers (Belzer et al. 2006). In fact, many groups have had trouble doing this over the last twenty to thirty years, although others have been fairly successful. The point, however, is that efforts to attract and keep the younger generation committed to their faith and involved in their congregations will inevitably bring about changes in the larger religious institutions.

This approach allows us to imagine what the future of religious groups may look like (and we would encourage studies of other religious traditions to see if the schema we have developed here might work, say, within Judaism or Islam) as they confront the challenge of making their faith relevant and accessible to the younger generations of believers. Also, we believe with Prothero, Winston, and even Dawkins and Harris that, as religion is one of the most important and, per Prothero, "volatile" variables in a globalized world, understanding how different groups approach their religious beliefs by implication provides a way for us to understand their approach to such larger issues as the kind of participation they encourage in the common culture, in the political and electoral process, and on larger social-moral issues, such as abortion, gay marriage, euthanasia, or other similar issues.

A related implication of our study is in how people are currently constructing identity and how they perceive and respond to legitimate authority. Post-Boomer conceptions of what counts as legitimate authority differs in significant ways from those of their parent's generation, and as such may signal coming change in the institutions in which Post-Boomers are active. Much of this is certainly embedded in the emerging global capitalist system, where one can construct an identity from a seemingly endless supply of consumer goods, as well as in the effects of the digital revolution on how we create, appropriate, and disseminate knowledge. This then ultimately determines who controls knowledge, and thus who has authoritative knowledge, which in turn implicates how individuals work within organizations and the kind of authority they see as legitimate within the organizations in which they are active, and that they might establish in the organizations they may create. This is important for both religious institutions as well as nonreligious institutions. That is, if individuals can construct almost any identity they might desire, and can create knowledge and legitimacy on their own without having to rely on more traditional means of authority, such as established organizations with their own systems of hierarchies and authority, what might that mean for the future of such societal institutions as politics, religion, and the family? It is conceivable, to bring this back to our specific interest in this book, that as Post-Boomers bring their own sensibilities about identity and authority into religious organizations, these organizations may undergo significant changes in authority structure and in what counts for legitimate knowledge and belief in the years to come.

These issues however are beyond the scope of this book and only serve to point up both the importance of understanding the next generation of religious believers and how their desires and demands may change the face of religion in America. Thus, in the remainder of this chapter, we want to lay out our basic understanding of how generations work and the particular life experiences that have been formative for Post-Boomers. Further, we will argue that Post- Boomers don't fit what we find in the literature on spirituality, and then introduce a new typology that we believe helps account for different types of approaches to spirituality. Finally, we will argue that a dominant theme that we find expressed in various ways across the typology is a new, emerging form of spirituality that will have a significant impact on how religion is understood and approached in the future.

POST-BOOMERS

Much has been written in recent years about the purportedly unique outlook of different generations in society, from the alienated "Generation X," to the more institutional friendly "Generation Y," to the ambitious "Millennials," and so on. As the expansion of generational labels has increased, the explanatory power of these ever more finely cut generational groupings has decreased, making it difficult to understand the essential differences between them. Further, these approaches, whether from members of these generations or from observers, treat each differently labeled "generation" as a monolithic entity that responds to different social and cultural stimuli in the same way across the entire group (on these themes see, e.g., Coupland 1991; Strauss and Howe 1991; Howe and Strauss 2000).

In contrast to these approaches, we present a more simplified generational conception that we believe holds more explanatory power, and that provides a better interpretive frame for understanding the ways that Post-Boomers are pursuing their spiritual needs and desires. Rather than trying to wrangle out the subtle differences between how one age cohort acts or is characterized as compared to others, we locate the experiences of Post-Boomers in significant social and cultural developments that they experienced in their formative years and then develop a typology of different responses to these cultural influences in their spiritual quest. Thus, just as the formative experiences of Baby Boomers were colored by such things as Vietnam, the "sixties," and in general a dramatic increase in their opportunities for individual expression, all of which resulted in a variety of responses from within that generation, so Post-Boomer's formative experiences were colored by developments unique to their time and place in history and we should expect that they would have a variety of responses to these experiences as well, rather than having a singular response to challenges of a changing culture (see Mannheim 1952 and Schuman and Scott 1989 for this basic framework on generations).

Although we have previously delineated several formative and shared experiences of Post-Boomers that have helped to shape their understanding of the world and how they approach their religious beliefs and commitments (Flory and Miller 2000), we would like to point out two that are of particular importance here, and then suggest two more as being particularly formative to the worldviews of Post-Boomers. First, perhaps the most obvious experience of Post-Boomers is that they are the children of the Baby Boomers, who went through the revolutions of the 1960s, and then raised their children accordingly. Of particular importance in this regard is the questioning of institutions in general that Boomers passed on to their children and a concomitant emphasis on the importance of pursuing one's personal journey, often without the benefit of any institutional affiliations (see Bellah et al. 1985).

A second cultural influence of the past several decades is subtler, but perhaps even more powerful. The world has become a global village. Post-Boomers grew up being exposed to multiple worldviews through media, schools, and in their own neighborhoods. For example, we expect that urban areas are populated with many different types of people, including immigrants from across the globe. However, this is also true in most suburbs today. What might be expected to be monochromatic suburban enclaves turn out to be fairly multicultural in reality, as urban and suburban areas are increasingly becoming one massive, sprawling geographic area, and immigrants are increasingly moving to suburban areas where there are jobs and good schools for their children. This increases the likelihood that children will grow up not only with friends of different races or ethnicities, but of different religious beliefs as well. Tolerance and acceptance of difference is thus a value for Post-Boomers, as their lives have been informed by many different perspectives and cultural understandings throughout their formative years.

Further, and related to globalization, the revolution in digital technology has provided access to multiple cultures and worldviews at the click of a button. This exposure has the potential to radically relativize our understanding of truth, or at least to reveal the social construction of belief and value systems. The current digital revolution has democratized access to information and images, and made that access interactive rather than passive. That is, digital technology, computers, cameras, cell phones (with cameras), and photography and filmmaking software are now relatively inexpensive and in widespread use. Further, rather than being passive observers of the products of these digital tools, people are now active participants in documenting their experiences and producing, reproducing, and manipulating images, disseminating ideas (through blogs and podcasts), sharing music, and the like. Thus music, television shows, and movies are all swapped through digital networks and uploaded to various websites, often with their content manipulated along the way. Digital cameras allow just about anyone to be able to make a movie, create a photo essay or exhibit, or just provide a more graphic way to display or sell goods (on the nature of the new digital media, see Manovich 2002; Stephens 1998; on the effects of digital media, see Burnett 2005; Hansen 2004; Ryan 2003; Tapscott 1998). Media theorist Douglas Kellner has argued that "a media culture has emerged in which images, sounds, and spectacles help produce the fabric of everyday life, dominating leisure time, shaping political views and social behavior, and providing the materials out of which people forge their very identities." It is this new media culture, Kellner argues, that shapes worldviews, defining "what is considered good or bad, positive or negative, moral or evil" (1995, 1).

A third formative influence is the failure and hypocrisy of corporate, political, and religious institutions to act ethically and in more than the most crass self-interest as they have pursued their own ends, often at the expense of their own employees and the public. Perhaps most obvious are the sex-abuse scandals among the priests in the Catholic Church, and also among evangelical ministers, where various sex scandals involving both heterosexual and homosexual activity have been uncovered. But there are also the many bribery and sex scandals of famous politicians, and of course corporate scandals that have ultimately brought about the failure of large corporations, costing people their livelihoods and their retirement savings, just so a few people at the top can enjoy even greater riches and status than they already do. As a result, Post-Boomers evidence a distrust and cynicism of large-scale institutions in that they are perceived to be completely self-interested and able and willing to manipulate public opinion in the service of their own selfish goals.

A final influence is what many have framed as the results of "postmodernism" in society. This is related to globalization and the resultant exposure to multiple worldviews and religious belief systems through friends, media, and educational institutions, and has led to the classic response, "whatever." That is, there seem to no longer be any universal truths, that what is true for one person may not be true for another, and it is all based on one's own experiences, whether through religion, lifestyle, ethnicity, or "whatever." This of course makes it difficult to maintain any sort of consistent religious belief system in one's life, and ultimately presents a significant challenge to religious institutions not only in terms of their own truth claims, but insofar as it becomes ever more difficult to attract and keep people in the fold.

POST-BOOMER SPIRITUALITY

These formative experiences have significant implications for Post-Boomers' approaches to religion and spirituality. Whether they are characterized as cynical toward or supportive of institutions, Post-Boomers do not tend to accept them unquestioningly. In our interviews and visits to different congregations and events, we have found that although Post-Boomers are willing to participate in religious institutions, they carefully choose the types of institutions within which they participate, they are more interested in the relationships and community that they find there than in the institution itself, and they can be somewhat fluid in their institutional commitments, often participating in more than one institutional setting at the same time.

Further, despite the fact that they live in a symbolically saturated culture, Post-Boomers have had as their primary religious experience a symbolically impoverished environment. Churches look like warehouses with little if any religious imagery, and worship is organized around passive audiences that might raise their hands in praise to God but rarely if ever interact with each other or the sacred in any form other than a sterile, cognitive recognition of the Other. In contrast, and often in reaction to this model, we have found that there are many within the Post-Boomer generation who are actively seeking religious experience in different ways from their parents' generation, from reinvigorating ancient symbols and rituals within their own religious traditions to borrowing from other traditions and even creating their own rituals and symbols in the service of an embodied spiritual experience.

Beginning with Robert Bellah's *Habits of the Heart* (1985), the dominant theme within the sociological study of spirituality in the United States has been the individual in pursuit of her or his own, often idiosyncratic, spiritual journey, especially as epitomized by "Sheilaism." This individualist theme has continued in such studies as Wade Clark Roof's investigations of Baby Boomer religion (Roof 1993; 1999; see also Carroll and Roof 2003) and Robert Wuthnow's studies of small groups (1994) and of spirituality since the 1950s (1998; 2001). Taken together, these studies suggest that, particularly since the 1960s, spirituality has become decoupled from religion, with many people pursuing their own private, individualistic, and noninstitutionalized form of spiritual fulfillment where the individual quest for meaning takes precedence over membership in, or commitment to, the religious community.

More recent work, however, has begun to show that there is more to the story of spirituality in America. Historian Leigh Schmidt (2005) has shown that the individualistic strain of spirituality that Bellah traces to Ralph Waldo Emerson, Walt Whitman, and the American transcendentalists has often included a commitment to public involvement, usually to progressive social and political goals, and can thus provide a model for linking spirituality and public involvement in the modern context. Similarly, Gregory Stanczak (2006) has identified an "engaged spirituality" where the individual has a personal spiritual commitment that includes active engagement in both transforming individual lives and larger social, civic, and religious institutions, and argues that an engaged spirituality functions to "permeate the boundaries" between the private/personal and the collective, and allows for "creative innovation for negotiating between private experience and public action or between spiritual transcendence and social praxis" (20).

The forms of spiritual quest that we describe in this book are more similar to the latter examples than the former, particularly in terms of Post-Boomers' commitment to a religious community within which they seek a physical experience of the sacred and actively live out their faith through participation in their congregations and in service to the surrounding community. Thus, this *embodied spirituality* is both personal and social—Post-Boomers seek individual spiritual experience and fulfillment in the community of believers, where meaning is both constructed and directed outward in service to others, both within the religious community and in the larger community where they are located.

This experiential, community/other-oriented spirituality makes sense in the context of what others have written about those we are calling Post-Boomers. For example, Richard Florida, in his study of "the creative class," which would include most Post-Boomers, certainly all we interviewed, emphasizes their pursuit of various experiences, not as spectators and not as in prepackaged experiences (such as tours, Disney, etc.), but as a product of their own creation (2002, 166–70, 182–87). Florida frames this desire as "experiential consuming," where "active, participatory recreation over passive spectator sports" is favored, and includes what he calls the "indigenous street-level culture—a teeming blend of cafes, sidewalk musicians, and small galleries and bistros where it is hard to draw the line between participant and observer, or between creativity and its creators" (166). Similarly, different studies of the interactive nature of digital technology and image representation/production show that the observer, or better the co-creator or even re-creator, can participate in the creation, re-creation, manipulation, and dissemination of various digital media (see Hansen 2004; Ryan 2003; Tapscott 1998).

A New Typology

Typologies of different forms of religious action in the world, such as Weber's soteriological typology of mysticism and asceticism (1993: 166–83), or H. Richard Niebuhr's five-part *Christ and Culture* typology (2001), which places different types of action on a continuum of resistance to cultural influences or accommodation to them, fail to capture the new empirical realities outlined above. For example, in contrast to what we might expect based on, for example, Niebuhr's typology, that Post-Boomers would represent a variety of types of either resistance to or accommodation with the larger culture, we have found that regardless of the particular way that Post-Boomers express their religious commitments, they are both, in Weber's categories, world rejecting and world affirming, and in Niebuhr's categories, they both resist and accommodate elements within the larger culture.

In contrast to these types of approaches, we have developed a typology of four emerging forms that exemplify the Post-Boomer spiritual quest, each a form of response to the challenges and opportunities they perceive to be represented in the larger cultural currents. The different forms, or types, that we describe present a more complex relationship between religious groups and their socio-cultural environment that we think is best expressed as a new typology of religious action.

Our first type, "Innovators," are those who represent a constantly evolving, or *innovating*, approach to religious and spiritual beliefs and practices. Many of these are newer, less established groups that are affiliated with the "emerging church" movement, while others are established churches and ministries that are innovating within their own traditions. These groups, whether emerging or more established churches, organize their approach (in contrast to what they see as an overly institutionalized and inwardly focused church), so as to focus on building community within the religious group and to engage in various ways with the larger culture. These churches are innovating by introducing various forms of ritual and symbol into their worship services and by introducing new forms of religious and community life that emphasize commitment and belonging, as well as service, within the religious congregation and to their host city.

Our second type, "Appropriators," refers to those churches and ministries that seek to provide a compelling and "relevant" experience for participants, both for those in the audience and for those who are performing in the service or event. In this, both churches and independent ministries seek to create these experiences through imitating, or *appropriating*, trends found in the larger culture and ultimately popularizing these through their networks into a particular form of pop-Christianity that is primarily oriented toward an individual spiritual experience. Appropriators tend to be situated within the mega/seeker church ideology, whether actually a part of a mega church or not. In fact, in many ways, each of the other three types we discuss in this book are at least in part responding to the form of Christianity represented by the mega/seeker model—a bureaucratized and consumption-oriented, franchised form of Christian expression and belief. Thus the mega/seeker church is the primary source, although Appropriators are found beyond those particular locations, and include Christian musical groups, consumer-oriented enterprises sponsored by and at churches, as well as retail stores and para-church ministries. But it is the desire for relevance and producing a culturally acceptable product mirroring the trends in the larger culture that drives this form of religious response to culture.

The third part of our typology is made up of what we call "Resisters," referring to what are primarily Boomer-initiated efforts intended to appeal to Post-Boomers by focusing on the recovery of "reason" and thus *resist* the incursion of postmodern culture within Christianity, hoping to reestablish the place of the written text and rational belief as the dominant source for Post-Boomer spirituality and practice. Resisters evidence several interrelated patterns within their perspective that represent different fronts in their continual efforts to identify and resist the various incursions of the larger culture that threaten the integrity of what they understand as historic Christianity. Each of these should be understood as both defensive and offensive patterns of response to the perceived threats, intended to provide resources for believers to defend against bad or improper beliefs in one's personal life, as well as more broadly within the church, and as strategies to fight for a particular religious and ideological perspective in the larger culture.

Our final type are the "Reclaimers," individuals who are all, in one way or another, seeking to renew their experiences of Christianity through the history, symbolism, and practices of ancient forms of Christianity, such as are still found in the liturgical traditions, particularly the Episcopal, Orthodox, and Catholic churches, thus *reclaiming* the ancient symbols, rituals, and practices of these traditions for their own spiritual quest. These are converts, either from other, nonliturgical forms of Christianity or from nonexistent or lapsed faith commitments. In this, the particular attractiveness of these traditions are the symbols, rituals, practices, and even smells of these churches, as well as the small congregational communities of believers that they represent, the connection to a larger historical tradition within Christianity, and the perceived authenticity that these traditions provide.

Methods

The research for this book was done over two years, and was initially based on some of the findings in our *GenX Religion* book, in particular the experiential dimension of GenX religious activities, their entrepreneurial skills at establishing new and culturally savvy organizations, the extent to which their religious identity is rooted in the religious community, and their emphasis on the "authenticity" of one's life, outlook, and religious faith as being a primary component of how they view themselves and each other. In this, we utilized several key informants that we had met either through our research for that project or as a result of our presentations and publication of the book and then began to follow the leads they provided us to both individuals and groups. As we visited and interviewed these initial contacts, we pursued a "snowball" sampling plan in which we asked them about other groups or individuals that they were aware of, and with whom we might interact. In addition, we sampled the Internet presence of the groups that we were contacting, and used a type of digital snowball sampling by following links on their websites and blogs to groups that they were referencing. This resulted in ten (physical) site visits and approximately one hundred interviews, all digitally recorded, both audio and video, and a significant sampling of a wide variety of Internet sources, from personal blogs to websites for different Christian groups. The sites we visited were located in different urban areas throughout the United States, focusing primarily on southern California, but also in St. Louis, Chicago, and New York.

Plan of the Book

In what follows, we devote a chapter to each of the four emerging types that we have identified, and have structured each chapter in the same way. In each of the chapters that describe the four parts of our typology (chapters two through five), we first describe an event or experience we had while doing the research that exemplifies the different characteristics of each type. Next we contextualize each type by providing some history and background to its development, and then we describe the characteristic approach and practices of each of the types. Finally, we provide a summary and conclusion that raises questions about different elements of the way that the type frames itself, or is pursuing its particular ends. We would note here as well that we have included a few representative photographs of each type within their respective chapters so as to provide a visual sense of what these types look like. The only exception to that is our Resisters chapter, where we have included no photographs. Our reasoning is that since Resisters are so adamantly resisting against an image-driven culture, it seems counter to their efforts for us to represent them visually.

In the concluding chapter, we compare and contrast each of the four parts of our typology, pointing up their commonalities, despite their obvious differences, and argue that we are seeing the emergence of a new religious type that we are calling "Expressive Communalism," in which Post-Boomers are seeking spiritual experience and fulfillment in community and through various expressive forms of their spirituality, both private and public. Expressive Communalism can best be understood in contrast to two classic theoretical types of religious behavior, Max Weber's "inner-worldly asceticism," in which the individual eschews emotional and sensuous enjoyment in favor of a rationally ordered life, and Robert Bellah's "utilitarian individualism," in which the individual seeks both material success and personal fulfillment. In contrast, in Expressive Communalism we find that Post-Boomers are seeking spiritual experience and fulfillment in embodied form through community, and through various expressive and experiential forms of their spirituality, both in their personal lives and in public, expressed in some way of "living out" their faith. In this, the individual finds personal spiritual fulfillment through a physical experience—whether visual, aural, or physical—primarily in the context of the religious community; however, the primary goal is not necessarily individual fulfillment, but living out, or embodying, their spiritual commitment publicly in the larger community through various types of service activities and cultural engagement with the community.

CHAPTER 2

Innovators

This is the church in the postmodern
context—living Christianity, not the doctrine or the institution, but getting back
to the simple way of following Jesus in a
complex time.

—Karen Ward, pastor, Church of the
Apostles, Seattle

VENTURA, CALIFORNIA

When entering the worship service at the
Bridge Communities, one is struck by all the activity that is
going on simultaneously, yet all organized around worship and
building community. There are digitally produced images pro-
jected on multiple walls of the space that are both visually
engaging and helping to provide a visual narrative to what is
happening at each part of the service. There are also various art-
works set on easels and hanging from the walls that have been
created for (or in) different services in the past. At the same time
the congregation might be singing, and several of the members
might be painting at easels set up around the room. The room is
full of round tables, with chairs set around the tables so that
people look at each other rather than having everyone facing the
front of the room all the time. At one point during the service
there is an extended sharing time in which the people seated at
each of the tables will exchange names, thoughts, concerns, and
prayer requests, which inevitably results in a shared prayer time

among the people seated at the table, or perhaps between two or three of those people. There is a time of teaching, usually not longer than about thirty minutes or so, followed by more singing, sharing a meal, and general socializing among the people of the church, all intended to create an atmosphere of community and belonging.

As well, the Bridge often creates an experiential atmosphere for their worship service that directs the members' experiences in a particular fashion. For example, at a recent Easter service they rented a large movie theater in downtown Ventura and transformed it into a "tomb" modeled on what a tomb might have looked like in Jesus' time period. As people entered the building, they were in effect entering the tomb, and when they exited, the idea was that it was as if they had risen from the dead, just as Jesus had. On another occasion, a fashion show was produced right in the middle of the worship service. Greg Russinger, who is the "lead missionary" (read pastor) of the Bridge, explained that the theme of the evening was "inner beauty," which in effect turned the logic of traditional fashion shows, which emphasize external beauty, on its head. For this, a couple of members of the congregation who were in school working toward degrees and careers as fashion designers were enlisted to produce items for the show that related to the theme of the evening, thus taking the talents of the members and using them in the service of the entire community. As the models— who also were members of the congregation—walked the run-way, to musical accompaniment as well as cheers and hoots of approval from the rest of the congregation, the designers were able to explain the pieces they had created and thus relate them to the theme of inner beauty.

But the Bridge isn't only cool music, candles, and an experiential worship setting; it is also a community that is intent on serving the needs of Ventura. They operate "AID," a program that includes several separate components, all oriented toward

2-1. A sharing time during a worship service at the Bridge Communities, Ventura, California. Photo by Richard Flory.

helping others in Ventura and showing their presence in, and commitment to, the city, and to demonstrate that everyone is welcome in their community. Some examples of their programs: "A trashcan can make a difference" is a theme-oriented collection program where items such as toiletries, canned food, baby articles, socks, or school supplies are placed in a trash can at the end of each month and then distributed by the church directly to those in need, as well as to agencies throughout the county that the church has formed partnerships with because of their greater distribution networks. Each Thursday evening, a group from the Bridge is in the downtown park, playing music, providing meals, playing with kids, and in general interacting with the local residents. The first Tuesday of each month, several people from the Bridge participate in a program that they call "Laundry Love," where they spend the evening doing laundry with and for the homeless of the city. They actually refer to the

2-2. Laundry Love volunteers (left) with homeless. The Bridge Communities, Ventura, California. Photo by Richard Flory.

homeless as "houseless" since, from their perspective, they have a home in the Bridge Communities, regardless whether they have a house or not. The evening includes lots of conversation, including the good-natured sharing of laundry tips, and relationship building as everyone waits for their laundry to finish. Through this program, genuine relationships have developed in that several of the "houseless" have come to be a part of the Bridge Communities in one way or another.

It is important to note that these programs at the Bridge only exist because one or another member of the church has a desire and commitment to initiate, organize, and maintain the program over the long term. Justin, a thirty-year-old financial planner for a large brokerage firm, who has been one of the organizers for Laundry Love, frames this approach, "There are two people that are paid staff at the Bridge. I came from a church with half the congregation size and ten people on staff. Everything is volunteer collaboration because there's just so much authenticity, I mean, I don't know, I've never been a part of something that wasn't so focused on bringing people into the church, but bringing the church to the people." This is precisely the approach that Greg Russinger desires for the Bridge Communities, and for Christian churches more generally, to no longer follow cultural trends in the effort to be relevant, but to lead culture by engaging in conversations with people outside of the church and learning from them, so that hopefully, in his words, he and the Bridge might "reveal to them who Christ is. The only way you can do that is by being in the middle of culture, having conversations, learning about where they're coming from and then beginning to speak into their life . . . not trying to create cool programs to somehow bring people in as much as to go out to where people are at. It's not 'Hey, why don't you come to the Bridge,' as much as 'Hey, we're the Bridge; we come to you.'"

LONG BEACH, CALIFORNIA

At Grace Church in Long Beach, California, we find a much different institutional context than at the Bridge, but a similar emphasis on an engaging worship experience and service to the community. Grace is a much older, and larger, church than the Bridge, having been founded in 1913, and owing to that history, it has a larger pastoral staff and a much more established congregational base, with many of its members having attended there for more than twenty or thirty years. In addition, it is in a fairly conservative evangelical denomination that has always prized itself on its emphasis on Bible teaching and a literal interpretation of the scriptures. In fact, before the church buildings and grounds were remodeled in 2001 to create a more welcoming atmosphere that is more conducive to interaction between church members and visitors alike, the motto on the sign at the main entrance to the church read: "The Bible, the whole Bible, and nothing but the Bible." The emphasis was on instruction from the Bible both in Sunday services and in the church programming. Over the past several years, however, that emphasis has expanded and developed as a vital and growing young adult population—roughly college age through their mid-thirties, including young families—has established itself at the church, much of it around the church's new vision for community development and arts development as a vital part of its identity.

Grace has also been able to take advantage of some of the elements of its own denominational identity and practices that show an elective affinity to the more visually and experientially oriented Post-Boomer generations. One example is their celebration of communion. Historically, the denomination has celebrated communion quarterly and in a fairly literal fashion, in a service dedicated completely to the communion service. In this, a type of re-creation of the Last Supper takes place; there is a sharing of food, the washing of feet, and the taking of the bread and cup. Traditionally for this church, the congregation was split up, with men in one part of the hall and women in the other part, and seating was relatively random at long tables, around which each of the participants would partake of the different elements of the communion.

The church, however, has adapted this service in recent years. Now it takes place once per year, at Easter, and the congregation is not split up, but rather families and friends sit together in smaller groupings so as to facilitate an experience shared with loved ones, in which the participants wash each others feet and share the bread and cup together. This reorganizing of the communion service has served to make the ritual reenactment more alive for those in the church, rather than its being simply a sort of ritualistic event that takes place out of duty or because of church tradition. This is at least in part due to the physically embodied aspect of the service that these young people seem to be seeking out. John Tubera, who as the director of artistic development was the staff member largely responsible for reconfiguring the communion service, noted that the young people in the church "resonate with the multiple sensory experience" of the communion, in particular because the three elements of the service—breaking bread together, washing of each others feet, taking the bread and cup—tangibly represent the incarnation of Christ, and what it means for them to be a Christian. That is, through these embodied acts toward each other, they are able to demonstrate love toward each other, serve each other, and perhaps reconcile strained relationships.[1] Thus Grace has managed to revise and innovate with a traditional element of its identity in order to make the communion service more meaningful to a new generation of members while maintaining and even enhancing the experience for the longer-term, older church members.

Within the last several years, Grace has also reconceived itself as a church that pursues its mission within a particular socio-cultural and geographical context, to serve "Long Beach [California] in the 21st century." As represented in the new vision statement, the church intends to "represent and extend the reign of God by making disciples of Christ in our city and, through our city, the world" (Vision to Reality: Celebration to Expectation, 2002–2003). Lou Huesmann, the senior pastor at Grace, says that the new vision emphasizes that "God has placed us here in Long Beach for a purpose, we're not just talking about evangelism, we're talking about serving the city, having Long Beach be glad that we're here as Proverbs talks about the city rejoicing. And so part of that means that we need to be part of the revitalization of this neighborhood and this city." For Grace this is represented in many different ministry programs, but for our purposes the most important are the social justice ministry "Hope for Long Beach" and the development of an extensive arts program. Each of these efforts is intended to "renew the culture" of Long Beach, and both are radically innovative within the context of the historic denominational affiliation and identity of the church, and are bottom-up ("organic") initiatives growing out of the concerns, interests, and desires primarily of the Post-Boomer community at the church.

It is important to note that these programs have been initiated and pursued on a somewhat larger scale than the similar programs at the Bridge; however, the impetus and intent are the same. Like the Bridge, Grace has made a conscious decision to have as its guiding vision a commitment to being a part of the life and culture of its host city. Thus through the art gallery, contemporary art shows are mounted from artists that may or may not be Christians, but whose art in some way resonates with matters of faith. In 2002, for example, a photographic exhibit of the large Cambodian community in Long Beach was mounted. The opening was simultaneously a celebration of the Cambodian community and the photographic exhibit itself. There were Cambodian folk dancers, a representative number of Buddhist priests, food, and of course the photographic exhibit, which remained on display for one month. The church's intent in mounting the show was in effect to demonstrate an openness and welcoming to the Cambodian community, while not downplaying their Christian commitments in the process. It was through this openness that Grace Brethren welcomed them to participate in and with the church. There is now a Cambodian congregation worshipping at Grace, as well as several other congregations, such as Indonesian and Spanish language congregations, due primarily to the community outreach efforts of the church.

Further efforts in the arts include regular exhibitions in the gallery, commissioned artists and interns such as painters, musicians and dramatists, and commissioned arts groups such as an actors' co-op, worship bands, and the like. The common theme across these many different activities is that the spiritual life is

a dark night of winter | ...the journey transformed...

2-3. Announcement for "A Dark Night of Winter," December 14, 2002, at Labrys Contemporary Arts Gallery/Grace Brethren Church, Long Beach, California. A multimedia arts liturgy featuring dance perform- ance, photographic and sculptural installation, spoken word, and song. Event planned by John Tubera, Jeff Rau, Meg Rau, Kurt Simonson, Alyssa Wiens, Johanna VanderBeek, and Kari Ryckebosch. Postcard design by Matt Maust. Photograph by Kurt Simonson.

not simply a cognitive affair, but that properly considered it must include the community, and one's physical body and all of its senses. For example, over the past several years, the church has organized an "arts liturgy" between Thanksgiving and Christmas. This has taken place on one weekend evening, with the organizers and participants from both the church and the community. The events have included several components, including liturgical dance, interactive sculptural and photographic installations, labyrinth walks, and singing and dancing among those in attendance and the performers/exhibitors. Huesmann admits that this has not been an easy task and that it is still a work in progress, but that the vision of the church is that in the "postmodern, post-Christian culture that we are becoming . . . I think the arts can be a tremendous way to speak to our culture about the beauty and integrity of Christianity," and that by developing in the artists associated with the church a "robust theological worldview that bears upon their art . . . we can speak to this culture in ways that the spoken word often finds limited."

CONTEXT

Churches like the Bridge Communities have been sprouting up, and others, like Grace Brethren, have been reconfiguring their ministries in ever increasing numbers over the past few years. These churches are located across the United States, and in many countries around the world, and all of them tend to speak the same language, as it were, emphasizing that the current cultural situation calls for a different type of Christianity that is more in tune with the larger culture. Many of them are linked together through the Internet, whether through websites, blogs, or email lists, which results in a global network of people and churches, many of whom know each other or are at least aware of each other's existence and what they are doing in their churches and ministries. Indeed, the availability of information about their activities through the Internet, as well as their documentation in many books, most of which have been published by leaders of these ministries since 2003, has provided access to many who would not consider themselves a part of any of these communities, regardless of whether they would be supportive of or opposed to their efforts.[2]

Connections/Networks

Although it would be impossible to enumerate the many and varied ways that different leaders, churches, and ministries come into contact with each other, there are two independent but related organizations, "Emergent" and "theooze.com," that provide excellent examples of how both networks of like minded individuals, churches, and ministries and the dissemination of information among them have been facilitated and developed within this type. Both of these organizations have a major and perhaps primary Internet presence, but they also organize and facilitate "real world" events, such as meetings, conferences, consultations, and the like.

Emergent was initially founded in 1996 as the Young Leaders Network by a small group of people who initially were seeking a form of Christian ministry that might be more relevant to "Generation X," yet within two years their generational ministry orientation was displaced by an emerging emphasis on the church and its mission in culture. Emergent, as this group has been known since 2001, is oriented toward a "missional," or outreaching, service-oriented Christianity in "postmodern culture," and has alternately been termed a community, friendship, network, conversation, and, more tentatively, a movement. Its leaders are primarily Christian ministry practitioners, whether lay or pastoral staff, and most of its Internet and real world activities are oriented toward being a resource and training ground for churches and church leaders who are, in their words, interested in pursuing and "imagining . . . new ways of being

followers of Jesus ... new ways of doing theology and
living biblically, new understandings of mission, new ways of
expressing compassion and seeking justice, new kinds of faith
communities, new approaches to worship and service, new inte-
grations and conversations and convergences and dreams."[3]
Emergent communicates with its affiliates through a regular
email newsletter (Emergent/C), and through its blog (emer-
gentvillage.com/weblog) and podcasts (emergentvillage.com/
podcast), and also sponsors various gatherings ("conversations,"
"gatherings," "institutes," "workshops," etc.) for ministry leaders and laypersons alike.

In 1998, Spencer Burke, formerly on the pastoral staff at
Mariners Church in Irvine, California, founded "theooze.com"
as a means to create a "safe place to ask questions and work
through issues" related to Christian belief and practice. This was
largely in response to his experience within Christian circles of
what he calls the "spiritual McCarthyism" that militated against
an open, questioning environment. Burke's idea behind the
name "theooze" is that "various parts of the faith community
are like mercury. At times we'll roll together; at times we'll roll
apart. Try to touch the liquid or constrain it and the substance
will resist. Rather than force people to fall into line, an oozy
community tolerates differences and treats people who hold
opposing views with great dignity. To me, that's the essence of
the emerging church" (Burke 2003, 36–37). Theooze.com is
essentially a clearing house of ideas about the current state of
Christianity that are being advanced by many different people
involved in these different types of innovative ministries. Many
articles are written specifically for theooze, others are culled
from across cyberspace, and as well, there are extensive links to
other innovative churches, ministries, blogs, and the like.

In addition to the online presence of theooze.com, Burke
and theooze have for the past several years organized "Soularize
(a learning party)," which is held in a different city each year,

and has included cities such as Seattle, Boston, Minneapolis, and Venice Beach, California.[4] Soularize brings together a roster of several leaders in the emerging church movement for workshops ("labs"), worship, study groups, a film festival, and social events intended to get those attending to network together and to develop relationships. In 2005, Soularize inaugurated a live webcast so that the event would not be limited only to those able to attend in person. As described on theooze.com, the webcast included live webcams and chats, along with postings of different aspects of the conference. As well, people were encouraged to host a study group or "lab" in their own community, inform the Soularize organizers about it so that they could post the information on theooze.com, and then "your learnings will be posted and archived along with those from the Venice Beach crowd."[5]

Not all churches that we would consider "Innovators" are directly involved in the emerging church networks, Emergent, or the different activities sponsored by these groups. However, the power of these digital networks is such that they have an effect not only on those who are directly involved, but also on the many "lurkers" who read and download the many different resources made available through the websites, or purchase the books and teaching materials that are produced from churches and leaders in these networks.

Writings

In addition to the virtual and real world networks that have developed among these churches, and despite the fact that much of the attention paid to these churches is because of their greater emphasis on the more visual and experiential, particularly in their worship services, many leaders in Innovator ministries have been publishing articles on websites, blogs, and in magazines, and a large number of books have been published by several people who have emerged in one way or another as leaders or spokespersons for this expression of Christianity. Although there are some key books that are popular and were formative to the thinking of Innovators that were not written by participants in these churches and ministries, by such authors as Lesslie Newbigin (e.g., *The Gospel in a Pluralist Society*), University of Southern California philosophy professor Dallas Willard (e.g., *The Spirit of the Disciplines*),[6] New Testament scholar N. T. Wright (among others, *The Challenge of Jesus* and *What Saint Paul Really Said*), and theologian Stanley Grenz (*A Primer on Postmodernism*), most have been authored by people who are involved in one way or another within these networks. The books by Innovator authors are not technical theological or philosophical writings; rather, they are more conversational in tone and are intended as resources both for individuals trying to come to terms with Christian faith in what is framed as a post-modern culture and for churches ministering in a postmodern culture. These books can be classified into two general cate-gories: theological interpreters of postmodern culture, and pragmatic descriptions of what is happening at a particular "postmodern" church or ministry, with the idea that it will be helpful to others who are traveling on the same path.

Among the theological interpreters of postmodern culture, Leonard Sweet, professor of evangelism at Drew University, published no less than eleven books on these themes between 1999 and 2007, and has become a theological guru of sorts for Innovators. His books are written in a type of pop-theology/ ministry style, complete with spellings of his name intended to connote his involvement with contemporary culture (for example, "Leon@rd Sweet"). His book titles seem to be intended to describe the turbulent, changing cultural context and how the church might minister within the digital, post-modern age (e.g., *SoulTsunami, AquaChurch, Post-Modern Pilgrims, Soul Salsa, Carpe Mañana*, etc.), Further, the books are often organized around easy to remember acronyms intended to capture the main ideas. For example, in his book *Post-Modern Pilgrims* Sweet uses each letter of the acronym EPIC (Experiential; Participatory; Image-driven; Connected) for each of the four primary chapters, followed by an "Endtroduction" to the book, all of which presumably suggests the postmodern theme of the book.

Similarly, Brian McLaren, a former English professor, founder and pastor of Cedar Ridge Community Church in Spencerville, Maryland, and currently, according to his biography on his website,[7] "a pastor, author, speaker, and networker among innovative Christian leaders, thinkers, and activists," as well as one of the more public leaders of Emergent, has become known as one of the most articulate and sought after apologists for a postmodern approach to Christianity. He has been sought out not only by other Innovator ministries, but also by the press as it tries to understand what exactly the "Emergent" movement is. He has made appearances on the PBS show *Religion and Ethics Newsweekly* (July 15, 2005) and was named one of the twenty-five most influential evangelicals in America by *Time* magazine in February 2005. McLaren published twelve books between 2003 and 2007, all of which articulate in some way what he has called "a new kind of Christianity." This new form of Christianity that McLaren writes of is alternately old and new, combining elements of ancient practice with a postmodern philosophical emphasis on story and narrative. McLaren's approach shuns a rationalistic, foundationalist philosophy of knowledge and knowing, and ultimately he has argued for what he has called a "generous orthodoxy," moving beyond "liberal" and "conservative/evangelical" Christianity, while taking seriously the claims of each (2004). He has gotten the attention of many Christian leaders, both conservative and liberal, with some mainline churches coming into the orbit of Emergent, some of the more conservative evangelicals becoming staunch critics of the whole program (see, e.g., chapter four, "Resisters"),

and others appropriating many of his—and other Innovators'—
ideas and practices in their own ministries (see, e.g., chapter
three, "Appropriators").

In addition to theological resource type books such as published by Sweet, McLaren, and others (see, e.g., Miller 2003;
2004; and Smith 2001), there has been a veritable explosion of
books authored by leaders from within different innovative ministries, representing ministries across the United States and in
such far-flung places as England, Australia, and New Zealand.
These books generally follow a similar plan: provide a description of the approach that a particular church takes toward worship, spiritual growth, and community outreach, which then
results in at least an implicit template for others to follow in
their churches. Thus, for example, Doug Pagitt, one of the original organizers of Emergent, and pastor of the Solomon's Porch
Community in Minneapolis, has published three volumes that
are based on experiences in and with his congregation, in which
he asks readers to "re-imagine church," to "re-imagine preaching," and to develop and cultivate "body prayer" (Pagitt 2004;
2005a; 2005b). Similarly, Greg Russinger, pastor of the Bridge
Communities, has published a book that is both a record of a
series of "conversations" between different ministry practitioners in meetings that the church has sponsored under the name
"The Soliton Sessions" and a sharing of those conversations
with a wider public (2005). The book not only provides a
record of different discussions on "faith, theology, leadership,
the church and missiology within the ever-changing and emerging global cultures," but provides questions and space, in the
form of blank pages, for readers to reflect on the questions
posed, presumably as an aid in both their own personal spiritual
development and in developing similar conversations at other
churches and ministries.

Jonny Baker and Doug Gay, leaders in the "Alt-Worship"
movement in the United Kingdom, have published a book

intended as a resource for new forms of worship that is organized around the major events in the Christian calendar, such as
Pentecost, Easter, Christmas, and Lent (2003). The book comes
with a CD full of music, videos, and still pictures, as well as text
for liturgy and instructions for rituals for each season. As
instructive as any of the resources included in the book and CD
is the introductory chapter of the book that outlines the development of the emerging church and alternative worship in the
United Kingdom. In this, Baker and Gay show the similarity of
the movement in the United Kingdom to the emergent movement in the United States, in that what is considered to be
emerging is not simply a new style of worship, but both a worship sensibility and an understanding of Christianity that closely
parallels the concerns and influences of the larger culture. Thus,
visuals, quick-cut videos, and club-type music accompany scripture readings and liturgies, and the inclusion in their theology of
such issues as environmentalism, social justice, and gender
equality signals a more significant shift than just a new worship
style. Finally, in New Zealand, Steve Taylor, the founding pastor
of Graceway Baptist Church in Elerslie, describes his book, *The
Out of Bounds Church?*, as a series of "postcards from the emerging church" that describe his journey of sorts through different
outposts of the emerging church (2005, 11). His is a journey
that is both descriptive of what other churches are doing, taking
full advantage of both digital and live networks of innovative
churches and leaders, and prescriptive in what churches can do
to better minister within the emerging postmodern framework.
He explores several questions that reflect the types of changes
he's observing, among them, "How could the notion of birth
and midwifery apply to the emerging church?"; "What is the
place of creativity in the emerging church and the implications
for our spirituality in a highly visual world?"; and "How is the
emerging church DJ-ing gospel and culture, mixing image and
sound, ancient and future, to create a remix for a new world?"

One final note about these books. Most, although not all, have been published by Zondervan Publishing, an evangelical Christian publishing house in Grand Rapids, Michigan, that has also published many volumes that are quite critical of the kinds of Christian expressions from these innovative churches. In fact, Zondervan has established the Emergent/YS imprint, under the auspices of which many of the emergent books have been published. In addition, in October 2005, Emergent announced that it had entered into two new publishing agreements, one a contract with Abingdon Press, an imprint of the United Methodist Publishing House, to publish a new series titled "Theology for the Emerging Church," and the other with evangelical publisher Baker Books to "develop a line of books for pastors and church leaders called emersion."[8] Thus, in what began, and in most cases has remained, as an approach that finds large-scale, "modernist" Christian institutions suspect at best, we find that many of the leaders of the most prominent examples of innovative churches and ministries are now also participating in mainstream corporate Christian publishing, which may not be all that innovative of an activity. We will return to this idea and what it might mean for the future of innovative churches and ministries in the conclusion to this chapter.

Ethos

Throughout all of these different sources, Innovators express several similar themes out of which their innovative approach to culture and Christianity develops. They are all in some way disillusioned or dissatisfied with the form of Christianity they have received, or that they see as otherwise lacking in authentic Christian character, and are seeking a more holistic approach to faith that combines both the cognitive and a greater sense experience of the divine, and are thus almost completely uninterested in rational, propositional expressions of their faith. They are seeking a community within which they

can pursue their faith commitments, and they conceive of themselves—or culture, or both—as postmodern and are wrestling with
how to be an "authentic" person of faith within that cultural
context.

Innovators, whether from a churched or unchurched background, tend to view the Christian churches and traditions
otherwise available to them as either out of touch with their
personal experience and with the culture they embrace or as
inauthentic appropriators of the culture. Karen Ward, pastor of
the Apostles Church in Seattle, frames this in comparison to the
large churches that have in many ways become the standard
against which most churches measure themselves, as a "going
back to the early [apostolic church] models, low maintenance,
stripped down, you don't need big buildings, big budgets, you
don't need a veneer, a staff of thousands, it's organic church,
do-it-yourself church, grow your own church."

It is likely no accident that most of the Innovators that we
interviewed, and those that are leaders in innovative churches,
are college educated, and in many cases graduate school educated, solidly middle class, and successful in their professional
lives. Thus the critical capacities they learned in college, as well
as the care and attention that they have paid to their careers,
make them in some ways bad candidates for following an
unquestioning "business as usual" approach to Christianity and
the church. What it makes them good candidates for amounts to
a partnership in the ministry of the church, rather than passive
consumers of the programs available in the church. Not only do
they look for opportunities to develop their spiritual lives in
their particular church communities, but also to serve others in
the larger community, usually through programs that are devised
and led not by a member of the pastoral staff, but by themselves.
Thus, contrary to what some studies have suggested (see, for
example, Hunter 1987), and despite what some may fear within
many Christian communities, the educational effect leads not to

a secularization of their beliefs, but to a more involved, critically engaged faith.

Much of this Innovator approach is framed in the context of postmodernity. Although there is not a standardized language among Innovators, they can be heard to be claiming that they are pursuing a postmodern faith, or a faith in the context of postmodern culture, or some similar formulation of postmodernity/postmodernism and the Christian faith. What this really means is not always clear, and sometimes, as in the often strained efforts of some writers to appear cool or "with it," this emphasis can seem more of a cultural posturing intended to position themselves and/or their churches as something uniquely different from other Christian churches. In general, however, there does seem to be a genuine difference in their approach and understanding of their faith. As Mark McLean of the United Church of Canada told us, "I think the people who are really starting to push the Gospel in directions that hasn't been seen before are the communities of faith that choose to be together, and those are communities of faith that may not be bound into churches, buildings, structures, the way its been done in the past, and that's when you enter into the postmodern discussion. . . . People from different theological perspectives, bioethical perspectives, denominational perspectives, to come together in worshipping in a community that's supportive in a very broad sense."

What this critically engaged, or in their terms "postmodern," faith looks like in innovative churches is a worship atmosphere that privileges sense experience and active participation over a more passive and cognitive worship, simultaneously creating new experiences, borrowing from other Christian traditions or even other faith traditions, and weaving it all together in original, innovative ways. In the life of the church community this takes on a much more communal "we're in this, and creating this, together" ethos than is found in the typical small groups that are organized in many churches that may provide a cohort of supportive friends, but not necessarily a commitment beyond that group. And developing community starts with the activities within the church such as worship services, reading groups, small groups, and the like, and then turns outward in service to their host communities. In this their search is for an "authentic" Christian faith that for them is relevant to all areas of life.

PATTERNS

We have identified this type as Innovators because of the constantly evolving, or *innovating*, approach to religious and spiritual beliefs and practices that these groups exhibit. As noted, many of these are newer, less established groups that are affiliated with the "emerging church" movement; others are established churches and ministries that are innovating within their own traditions. These groups, whether newer "emerging" churches or more established ones, frame their approach in contrast to what they see as an overly institutionalized and inwardly focused church, seeking instead one that is focused on building community, both within the religious group and with the surrounding community, and engaged in various ways with the larger culture. These churches are innovating in terms of their responses to the larger culture, introducing various forms of ritual and symbol into their worship services and creating new forms of religious life that emphasize community and belonging, as well as service both within the church and to the larger community.

From among the congregations we visited and through our interviews, we have found four primary characteristics that describe the innovative efforts of these churches and ministries. First, there is a prevalence of visual representations and expressions of the sacred; second, most of these congregations tend to be small in size and high in commitment; third, there is a general disinterest in established institutional forms of religion; and fourth, there is both an inward experience and an outward expression of the spiritual.

Visual Expression and Representation

One of the first things you notice as you enter the space occupied by one of these groups is their emphasis on the visual representation and expression of the sacred. This can include some forms that are more traditionally religious, such as crosses or icons, but more typical are the paintings, computer-generated visual effects, photographs, and three-dimensional images that do not necessarily appear to be religiously oriented at first glance. These are often expressions of spiritual seeking or experience and can be as easily completed during a worship service as they can be created beforehand to be used in the service, or perhaps as an exhibit in an art gallery that the church might operate. This emphasis is the result of the church's success in attracting members who are conversant with and actively involved in cultural industries such art, design, and film. This is not to say that everyone who attends one of these churches is an artist or filmmaker, rather that there is a valuing of a visual aesthetic as a way to express and experience spiritual things.

For Greg Russinger at the Bridge Communities, the atmosphere created by all the visual images and narrative, and any artwork that may be created for or within the worship service, is not about putting on a show for others to watch. It is instead an integral part of the larger efforts at the Bridge to provide a context for people to talk with each other and to connect with God:

> . . . it's amazing when people begin to share life through paint, clay, sketching, whatever the case may be. The conversation that gets birthed from that is magical, I think. The reality that one can open up through the dynamic of what one has created, allowing other people to come in to

talk with them about their life. I can come alongside and ask them, "Why did you use that color? Why did you paint the way you do? What is that telling me about who you are?"

It is through this process of using artistic forms of expression to create conversations that they can "investigate the mystery of the gospel" in ways that words alone don't allow.

Visual art also has a significant role at Grace Church in Long Beach, primarily through their active art gallery and associated programming. The church has developed a program that includes regular exhibitions in the gallery and commissioned artists and interns, such as painters, musicians, and dramatists, all emphasizing the theme that the spiritual life properly considered is not only a cognitive affair, but must include the body and all of its senses. Pastor Lou Huesmann argues that "it begins with creation, with God as creator," which opens up the possibility for art. He says that the church community has been shaped by the "simple paradigm, creation, fall, redemption, restoration . . . which has then been the umbrella under which the arts have developed" at the church. Ultimately, he sees the arts as a way to speak in a different way to current cultural sensibilities: "My ultimate vision for all this is that in a culture like ours, you know, postmodern, post-Christian that we are becoming, especially here in southern California, I think the arts can be a tremendous way to speak to our culture about the beauty and integrity of Christianity."

Small in Size, High in Commitment

In contrast to the large, "seeker" or "mega" church model that has been the dominant form in the United States for the past thirty years, these churches are often intentionally small so as to facilitate a greater sense of community through more intensive face-to-face interaction. For most, their desire is not to grow for the sake of growing, but to limit their size so that they can in some way create the type of religious and spiritual community that promotes a sense of belonging to something bigger than just themselves. This is in part a reaction to the mega church phenomenon, in which there seems to be a ministry for every life stage—a format that can be somewhat alienating due to the sheer size of those congregations. It is also related to the desire among Innovators to have a personal connection with others in their religious community and to have more direct participation in the different programs of the church and in its overall mission. Greg Russinger, who told us of his goal to split the Bridge into different congregations once the church got to 250 members, put it this way: "I don't really see Jesus, you know, having a score card or a belt to put the notches [counting the number of church members]. Why do we live in the realm of church culture where the first question that comes up about church life is how many people are you running? Shouldn't it be how many people have you invested in this week? How many people have you engaged? I come from the philosophy of belief that I will never get caught up in the dynamic of largeness because I think largeness is not numbers as much as it's largeness of heart and what lives have been changed."

Andrew Jones, who works with several organizations throughout North America, Australia, Asia, and Europe "in support of young people doing ministry in emerging culture" suggests that this denotes a value shift in how church ministry is being approached. He says, ". . . much of the ministry that we were trained to do and we have been reproducing over the last few years, few decades, has been based on a very modern worldview and a modern value system, which values things according to how long they lasted and how big they could become and the kind of impact and, actually, what's more institutional rather than relational or personal and not necessarily open to the supernatural or to spiritual things." What he has seen develop over the last few years are instead churches that are more "organic and local, committed to a local expression that's unique and makes sense for that smaller group of people. Everywhere it seems that if we really value intimacy and powerful worship experiences that are fully interactive and if we value community on a deep level where we're really sharing life together and secrets and money, then we're looking at smaller groups than we're used to seeing."

Uninterest in Institutions

Related to the emphasis on small size, we find a consistent and significant lack of interest in the institutional/organizational demands that larger churches must support. Most of these groups do not own any physical plant, rather they might rent or lease a building or a room that they can use one or two days per week, or they might have struck a deal with a local pub or coffeehouse that allows them to meet weekly. Further, they pursue these arrangements by design—they are not particularly interested in owning real estate, or building large institutional settings for their churches, or having, as Karen Ward of the Apostles Church termed it, "a staff of thousands," and programs to match.

The Apostles Church provides a good example of this approach. Church members meet in "micro-churches" in various homes in the city throughout the week, and then come together each Saturday evening for a "mass gathering" of worship, sharing together, partaking in a common meal, and then going back into the community. Similarly, the Bridge originally met in a rented space in a light industrial area of the city, and then moved into an old American Legion building in the downtown area once it became available. The draw of the new location was the downtown area, the kitchen in the building from which they could provide community meals, and the central location for the community within the city.

A further indicator of their lack of interest in and commitment to institution building is the size and conception of their ministerial staff. As with the congregation size, generally the staff is small as well—usually a lead person, and perhaps a support person. Although the lead person may from the outside appear to function as a "pastor," this is not necessarily the term by which they are known, nor do they necessarily conceive of themselves as "the person in charge." Rather, they often operate as facilitators of both the religious experience of the congregation for any given meeting and the overall direction of the group, but even this can be understood as a function of the religious community. As Andrew Jones has observed, "The kinds of churches we're seeing are very organic, very decentralized. . . . They don't need a senior pastor. In some ways it's more like the early church in the book of Acts where you had elders, you had leadership and you also had wandering apostolic people speaking into different churches . . . but you didn't have the business world, or outer structure, or all the priestly structure."

This makes for a relatively noninstitutionalized and non-hierarchical authority structure for the community, which is not to say that these churches do not have elders or deacons, or other spiritual leaders, rather that even the way that they are organized is based on what they conceive as spiritual gifts and abilities rather than the requirements of the organization. For example, the Apostles Church website[9] describes its leadership this way: "Church of the Apostles is a community led by the Holy Spirit (Romans 8:14). We take seriously our birthing as children of God (by water and the spirit), and our royal priesthood (as disciples of Jesus Christ). Within a body of believers, God always provides those who have the *charisms* (gifts) of tending, nurturing, teaching and guiding." Following this explanation is a listing of several persons in the church, all of whom, with the exception of the pastor, are laypersons in the congregation.

Inward Experience/Outward Expression

The inward experiential and outward expression of the spiritual takes two primary forms: first, in the personal and corporate experience of worship services, and second, in how the worshippers conceive of living out their religious commitments within the surrounding community and culture.

First, regarding the worship service itself, there are generally a variety of experiences that can take place, each of which emphasizes and requires the interactive and physical, rather than the passive and (primarily) cognitive. There likely are many things taking place simultaneously; music and singing, opportunities for personal expression of one's spiritual experience such as painting, or prayer stations, scripture readings, sharing in small groups within the larger service context, and the like. There is an order and structure to the service, but the emphasis is on both personal experience and expressing what that experience is to others within the community. At the Bridge, the services have what Greg Russinger calls a "textural" quality: "Worship is not a vocal thing. Partly it's vocal but it's a very whole dynamic, it's very physical, either the expression of one's body through the brushing of paint, through the reading of poetry, we always allow moments engaged in song. We never put a minute to it, twenty-five minutes of this, thirty minutes of that, as much as it ends when God says it should end. And then we allow people to respond through what they've created, to talk about what that worship was for them. So, a lot of texture to it."

Second, for each of these groups, their conception of living out their particular religious commitments has not been limited to simply having religious and spiritual experiences and sharing them with each other. Rather, they have all, in one way or another, conceived of their responsibility and desire to live out their beliefs in the context of the surrounding/supporting community in which they are located. So, we hear them constantly talking about being "in the middle of culture" or of "serving the city," which means that they are not just getting together to share in a common religious experience, but rather that they are developing various programs and outreaches to their host neighborhood/town/city. For example, when he first arrived at Grace, the church was, according to Lou Huesmann, "inward focused." One of the goals through their different programs in the arts and community activism has been to live out their commitment to the idea that Grace is to fulfill God's purpose for the church through its service to the city of Long Beach, through attempting to meet spiritual needs and physical, social, and cultural needs. Similarly, the goal at the Bridge is to be, according to Greg Russinger, like "a rock that is dropped into water and it creates this circular rhythm of change. Our life in Christ should be that same dynamic of being in the midst or the middle, the center of culture beginning to change [the culture]" through their involvement in and services to their cities.

Innovators have found sources for the embodiment of their religious experience through various means, ranging from the use of new digital media to being active in small religious communities. In each, Innovators find an embodied spirituality by physically expressing and/or experiencing spiritual fulfillment, whether through painting, sharing in community together, or through serving others as an expression of their spiritual commitments.

SUMMARY AND CONCLUSIONS

Innovators demonstrate a desire for embracing the "emerging" postmodern culture, and within that context are engaging in a spiritual quest that by definition is one that must change and adapt—innovate—to meet the changing cultural currents. Through our interviews and visits to their churches and events, three characteristics seem most important in providing a summary of their spiritual quest. First, they embrace the body as a locus for an active, experiential spiritual life. For Innovators, simply knowing what they believe is not sufficient for their needs and desires; rather, they actively seek to use their bodies in their spiritual activities. Second, they are committed to smaller, more intimate religious communities rather than seeking to grow and develop into larger institutional structures. They seem to have no ambitions to build the large structures and staffs that are a staple of the American religious scene, and they exhibit a realization that the communities that they create may in fact have their own life span, including when they may cease to exist. Finally, they are not content to seek refuge within these small, intimate religious communities; rather, they seek to serve the larger communities in which they are located. They are, in the words of some of our Innovators, more interested in "bringing the church to the community" than they are in bringing the community to the church.

Certainly something Innovators are doing is touching a chord within the Christian church. Their effect on worship and the different responses and critiques they are receiving from different segments of Christianity are telling, in that not only are other churches picking up on the form of their worship, with lots of candles, couches, and various visual and experiential elements being introduced, but they are generating a good deal of critique, particularly from the more conservative segments of Christianity. Further, although it is difficult to estimate the number of churches and ministries that can be framed as Innovators, it is clearly a growing and vibrant development that has emerged in many different parts of the world. Whether this continues to be an innovative development within Christianity over time remains to be seen, and brings to mind several questions and observations in this regard.

First, as Innovators institutionalize their networks, and as they are more mainstreamed in their efforts through speaking engagements, media appearances, book and article publications, and the like, can they sustain their vitality in the long run, or will their innovation become routinized into the very thing they are seeking to reform? Further, to the extent that they can maintain the human scale of their efforts, will they be more likely to survive and innovate into the future, or, as Andrew Jones has suggested, will they simply die off as any organic body naturally does once its life span is over? Already, however, it seems that much of the "emergent church" is already being corporatized and institutionalized through the very networks and sponsorships that they have developed and pursued. To take just one example: as noted previously in this chapter, many of the emerging church leaders have moved well beyond their church and ministry websites and their personal blogs to publish books—most of these with Zondervan Publishing, an evangelical Christian publisher and subsidiary of Rupert Murdoch's News Corporation, which publishes a wide range of Christian books, including many by authors who are very critical of the emerging church movement. This relationship between the Innovators and their publishers, and by extension their critics and fellow travelers, does not necessarily mean that their most creative or innovative ideas and work will be subjected to corporate control; however, it is one sign of a broadening network of relationships that include much that they have been critical of in their work, in particular a close involvement with the very structures of the institutionalized Christianity they critique, and of course the attendant "star power" of various authors such as Brian McLaren, Leonard Sweet, and others that results from such media and critical exposure.

On the other hand, there is at least some evidence that Innovators are willing to maintain their commitment to small, organic communities of faith instead of developing large institutional structures. For example, just as we finished writing this book, we heard that the Bridge Communities in Ventura was no longer together. When we contacted Greg Russinger, we found that the story of the Bridge and its end was much more interesting than that they just quit meeting together. The Bridge "lived" for eight years and had been very successful in achieving the mission that it had set out for itself. Yet as the church developed and matured, its leadership realized that in order for it to continue to be truly "missional," it would, according to Greg, "need to die so it could re-imagine itself." So the members of the church took it through a "death process" in which the community celebrated what it was and had become, a process that took several months and concluded in December 2006.

Following the death of the Bridge, a core group of people from the church have remained together, now calling themselves the "Symbol People,"[10] and are currently embarking on a process of thinking through what it means to be a community of Christians who are organized around four symbols: Christ, Community, Compassion, and Creativity. They meet together regularly, although as Greg said, they are "decentralized," and "pretty mobile," meeting at different members' homes, pubs, parks, the beach, or other similar places, having given up their downtown Ventura building. They are traveling light, as it were, without the institutional requirements that they had developed in their previous incarnation. Their goal in "putting to death" the Bridge and then starting new with a smaller, core community was to "reimagine" their mission as a church and to become something new in the future, within the context of seeking what it is they believe God wants them to be.

Although it is impossible to say with any accuracy what will happen to our Innovators in the future, we see that there are at least three possible outcomes, each of which are, from our perspective, equally plausible. First, Innovators may make their presence known within Christianity for several years, and then either just run out of gas and cease to exist or, like the Bridge/ Symbol People, continue to "reimagine" their mission and create new institutional forms over time. As Andrew Jones has

suggested, this should be expected since most of these organizations, at least at this point in their development, view themselves
as organic bodies that *should* have a natural life span of birth, life,
and death. Their death then would presumably lead to other
new developments in their quest to be as "authentic" as possible
within their communities and through the resources available to
them. It seems plausible then, that if they remain true to their
noninstitutional beliefs, we should expect cycles of birth and
death of innovative types of churches and ministries, perhaps
like the example of the Bridge/Symbol People.

The second possible outcome would be that the Innovators are successful, but their success leads to their becoming
co-opted by mainstream Christianity, thus simply becoming part
of the larger world of Christianity within their own traditions.
As their networks have expanded to include more mainstream
Christian groups and their experiences have become known
through their publications, their efforts may be turned into
models for other churches to follow, thus undercutting the
innovative nature of their efforts and making them just another
group within Christianity. Indeed, the popularity of the books
by Innovator writers such as Leonard Sweet, Brian McLaren,
and others would seem to be equally positive and negative in
terms of Innovator ideals. On the positive side, to the extent that
they are able to convince others of the importance of their perspective, they will likely help create further innovation over
time. On the negative side, it is entirely possible that their ideas
will be taken and introduced into the very structures that they
are moving away from, but in form only—atmospherics such as
candles, couches, and lava lamps—losing the content along the
way. Spencer Burke, of theooze.com, told us that the risk is
always present that as soon as some new development is perceived as "the new model" for ministry, it will be quickly copied
and disseminated through many different Christian ministries,
while losing its original vitality along the way.

The third possible outcome would be that the Innovators might actually create and maintain something that is a genuinely different expression of Christianity, and at least lay the groundwork for an alternative to the liberal mainline and (predominantly) conservative evangelicalism. What this would look like is still a matter of conjecture, and most of those whom we have identified as Innovators would tell us the same thing. What is certain, however, is that if something new develops and has any sort of staying power, it will be less dogmatically liberal or conservative, and more oriented toward an embodied spiritual practice and experience, including both personal experiences as well as outreach and service commitments, while not downplaying the importance of theological beliefs, but emphasizing that belief is simply the starting place for a much larger commitment to Christianity. This, it would seem, is actually the goal of each of the churches and ministries we have been framing as Innovators, yet, there are no guarantees for them that this will actually work out in the long run. As a cautionary tale for Innovators, one can look to the originally innovative efforts of Chuck Smith and Calvary Chapel in the 1960s, which now has over fifteen thousand affiliate congregations around the world and enforces a strict adherence to a conservative theology and politics that is now representative of much of Christianity in America.

CHAPTER 3

Appropriators

They will know us by our T-shirts.
—From a blog by the same name, maintained
by "Ben," of Portland, Oregon

ANAHEIM, CALIFORNIA

As we drove up to Anaheim Stadium—where Major League Baseball's Angels play—we were wondering what this particular evening would look and feel like. We were on our way to the annual Harvest Crusade, held for three nights each summer since 1990 at the home of the Los Angeles Angels of Anaheim.[1] The Harvest Crusade is modeled after such large-scale events as the Billy Graham Crusades, which themselves are modeled after similar evangelistic crusades held over the last 150 years by such preachers as Dwight Moody, R. A. Torrey, and Billy Sunday, and are led by pastor and evangelist Greg Laurie of Harvest Fellowship in Riverside, California. Yet the program for this particular night of the crusade was especially organized and promoted as the "Harvest Jam Youth Night," complete with special bands and freestyle motocross riders. It was this last aspect that we were trying to figure out as we approached the stadium. What exactly did freestyle motocross riders have to do with an evangelistic crusade, whether or not it was billed as the "Harvest Jam"?

Beginning in the spring each year, it is almost impossible to miss the fact that the Harvest Crusade will be happening and when it will take place, with the ubiquitous Harvest Crusade bumper stickers seeming to adorn every other car on the southern California freeways. Each year the Anaheim crusade draws upward of one hundred thousand people over the three nights, and on this night the official attendance was forty-eight thousand—a standing-room-only crowd.[2] We paid the $10 parking fee, which was collected by the stadium parking concession, and as we walked across the parking lot we saw several families enjoying a "tailgate" barbeque dinner prior to the start of the evening's festivities, several booths set up promoting various Christian radio stations, Christian bands, and the like, and even some protesters who carried signs that read "Laurie Leads to Hell." The line of people waiting for the gates to open snaked around the entrance and down the first base side of the stadium. We worked our way through the crowd to the media entrance— we had secured media passes so we could move around the stadium, take pictures, and talk with people without constantly having to explain ourselves, which also allowed us to enter the stadium without waiting in the long line. Having media passes was like having backstage passes to a concert—we could go pretty much wherever we wanted to go, including on the playing field (stay off the infield grass please!), and whenever we encountered one of the hundreds of volunteer ushers, we were asked, "How are you?" and ushered past any barrier intended to keep crusade attenders from going beyond. The Harvest Crusade is a big production that requires an office and staff at the Harvest Fellowship church in Riverside dedicated solely to organizing these crusade events, as well as a large contingent of volunteers from area churches who act as ushers, sell Harvest-related merchandise, and in general help direct people where they need to go both inside and outside the stadium.

As we entered the gates and went into the concourse (the area just outside the stadium where normally beer, pretzels, and hot dogs would be sold during a baseball game), we found that the entire area was taken up with booths, essentially temporary retail stores, each selling all sorts of Harvest-themed items: sweatshirts, hats, wristbands, jewelry, books (most authored by Greg Laurie), stickers, pins, CDs, DVDs, and of course T-shirts. Everywhere we looked there were T-shirts for sale, being worn by those walking through the stadium gates, and special Harvest Crusade T-shirts being worn by the crusade volunteers. There were T-shirts emblazoned with various Harvest logos and designs that looked just like T-shirts available at any surf or skateboard shop in the area, and T-shirts that appropriated various pop-cultural sayings, events, and icons, each promoting a Christian message. One notable shirt we saw was modeled after the "Vote for Pedro" T-shirt from the movie *Napoleon Dynamite*, complete with the same red-colored font and navy blue trim, that said "Jesus Died for Pedro."

In addition to the official Harvest Crusade products for sale, each of the bands that were to provide the musical entertainment for the evening had several booths set up to sell their T-shirts, wristbands, buttons, hats, CDs, DVDs, and jewelry. And as if that weren't enough, there were a couple of booths for a Christian retail store, C28, which has stores in several malls in southern California and has recently established franchise sites as far away as Florida, that were also selling T-shirts, stickers, buttons, wristbands, CDs, and DVDs.[3] In addition to all of that, there were several Christian media outlets, such as radio, television, and movie production companies, each with booths set up to advertise their different shows and products. These groups, in an effort to advertise their products to the masses attending the crusade, were giving things away. Usually they were small items, such as bookmarks or key chains emblazoned with their company logo, but one local radio station, "Kwave, the wave of living water," was giving away free T-shirts. Needless to say, the line in front of their booth was the longest of any we saw.

The bands for Harvest Jam were "Kutless"—the significance of the name is that in his death, Jesus took their cuts for them, leaving them "Kutless," although it is not clear why the "K" instead of a "C"[4]—is a Christian rock band that plays "melodic rock" and sounds something like a cross between Creed and Limp Bizkit, complete with the occasional growling and completely unintelligible lyrics; Toby Mac, a blue-eyed blond young man who is a former member of the Christian rap group DC Talk, who was dressed in appropriate urban/ghetto clothing; and Jeremy Camp, who all the young girls went wild for (Jeremy! Oh Jeremy!!!) and who had the complete "metrosexual" look with frosted highlights in his hair, earring, tight black T-shirt and jeans, tribal tattoos encircling his biceps, and whose music was a sort of cross between acoustic pop and melodious hard rock. In other words, the music sounded exactly like what one might hear on pretty much any popular music radio station or at a rock concert or on any of the iPods owned by those in attendance, and in fact seemed completely modeled on what was current on the music charts and with popular tastes.

Once inside the stadium, the scene was almost surreal. A large stage was set up, centered over second base and facing home plate. There were seven large projection screens on the stage, all projecting different images, messages, and advertisements for various crusade-related items. Huge speakers were on each end of the stage, with a small podium in the middle. Beyond the stage, the crusade was utilizing much of the stadium's multimedia capabilities, with "Welcome to Harvest Crusade" and other messages being shown on the electronic billboard on the face of the stands, while other images were being shown on the huge stadium video screen over the outfield stands. On the roof of each dugout were large, professional-grade video cameras and tripod rigs for broadcasting the event on television and on the web. Alongside all of the multimedia announcements and images specifically about the crusade, there were the permanent advertisements for a variety of stadium sponsors, including the fast food chain Carl's Jr., Budweiser, Bud

3-1. Greg Laurie preaching at the Harvest Crusade in Anaheim, California, in July 2006. Used by permission from Harvest Ministries with Greg Laurie, P.O. Box 4000, Riverside, CA 92514.

Light, Toshiba, and Chevrolet, as well as banks, mortgage companies, cell phone companies, grocery stores, real estate developers, and even an area casino owned and operated by a local band of Native Americans. All of this made for a strange juxtaposition of marketing, one set of advertisements for beer and hamburgers and gambling, and the other for Harvest Crusade and Greg Laurie.

And make no mistake, Greg Laurie was being as aggressively marketed as any other product at the crusade. From the Harvest Crusade website to the bumper stickers to virtually every public mention of the crusade, his name was attached in equivalent size font, as though it were the complete name, "Harvest—Greg Laurie," and with his smiling face nearly as ubiquitous.[5] As everyone was filing into the stadium and finding their seats, there was a constant stream of advertisements for various Greg Laurie products—books, videos, CDs, DVDs, and even a documentary, "*Lost Boy: The Greg Laurie Story* (coming in 2006)."[6]

All of this was streaming in a loop on all of the screens and through the stadium sound system until the evening's program began, and then, in between different acts, it ran again. On the off-chance that you might not have noticed all the images promoting and selling the different products, there was a disembodied voice that in its best radio announcer style would regularly accompany one or another of the advertisements, saying things like, "What is truth?" "Do you know where you will spend eternity?" and "When will the world end?" These were always followed up with the assurance that "Greg Laurie helps you to find out," whether in his new book, or his new CD, or his new DVD, and everyone was encouraged to "Get Your Copy Today!"

Following sets by Kutless and Jeremy Camp, the freestyle motocross riders started their show. Freestyle motocross has been popular for many years, particularly with the X Games promoting these sorts of "extreme sports," and has been a part of Harvest Crusade since 2003. Essentially, freestyle motocross consists of off-road motorcycles ("motocross bikes") and large ramps, which are used to shoot the rider sixty feet from takeoff to landing, thus enabling the rider to maneuver his motorcycle into some sort of airborne "trick" and hopefully land on the neighboring ramp without crashing. As the motocross riders started their bikes and the whine of the engines and smell of the exhaust permeated the stadium, the crowd started cheering. The riders came into the stadium from the right field bullpen and proceeded to ride their bikes around the dirt warning track that surrounds the grass field, around the outfield, down the left field foul line, and behind home plate, straightening out for the run up to the ramp, and then gunning the accelerator quickly up the ramp and flying through the air—both rider and motorcycle.

As the motocross riders zipped around the field and up and over the jumps, the announcers, who sounded more like they

3-2. A stadium motocross rider at Harvest Crusade. Photo courtesy of Harvest Crusades. Used by permission from Harvest Ministries with Greg Laurie, P.O. Box 4000, Riverside, CA 92514.

were from professional wrestling than announcers at a religious gathering, got the crowd even more excited, encouraging them to cheer every trick performed by the riders. The tricks in fact demand both skill and courage, as the riders, while flying through the air, are doing flips, letting go of the handlebars, flying like superman, twisting, turning, "grabbing" the handlebars with only their feet, with just enough time at the end of their trick to straighten out the motorcycle and land on the ramp to go around and do it again. It was a constant barrage of loud motocross engines and over-the-top announcers who excitedly described each trick the riders performed: DID YOU SEE THAT, BOB?! A BACKFLIP NAC-NAC TO HEEL-CLICKER TO NO-HANDER LANDER![7] WOW! THAT HAS NEVER BEEN PERFORMED BEFORE AT HARVEST CRUSADES!! And, as if on cue, the crowd went crazy with each jump, and even crazier when the announcers got them going with their descriptions. UNBELIEVABLE! In addition, the announcers also provided descriptions of each rider, informing the crowd that one rider was the WORRRLLLD CHAMMMPIONNN! That for another, THIS IS HIS MINISTRY!

The final act of the evening wasn't any one of the bands or even the WORRRLD CHAMMMPION MOTOCROSS RIDERS FOR JESUS!, but Greg Laurie himself, which after all the excitement of the bands and the jumping and flipping motorcycles was only slightly anticlimactic. At least for us. For pretty much everybody else in the stadium, all the entertainment was just that, good, clean (and free) Christian entertainment suitable for everyone in the family. What they really wanted to see, or more precisely hear, was Greg Laurie preaching his "clear, relevant gospel message," on this night, answering the question, "Are we living in the last days?" And although Greg Laurie and his sermon are clearly intended to be the centerpiece of each evening of the crusade, including the night of the Harvest Jam, watching and listening to him preach from the middle of a professional sports arena, surrounded by his own advertisements and all the marketing for beer and restaurants and casinos, was an experience with a fair amount of cognitive dissonance—at least for us. Everyone else loved their time at the Harvest Crusade, and apparently saw no contradictory elements in the fusion of Protestant Christianity with marketing, promotion, sales, and blatant cultural appropriation, both of style and substance. Yet despite our observations, and perhaps this is the most remarkable thing, the crusade was by any measure a success; over one hundred thousand people attended over the three days of the crusade, with 8,540 of them leaving their seats in the stadium to go onto the field to "make decisions for Christ."

In the end, it is difficult to determine why everyone was at the crusade. Although the primary goal of the crusade was to convert people to Christianity, or perhaps to motivate Christians to "rededicate their lives," all of the people we spoke to were

Christian believers who attended church regularly, and thus were not the apparent targets of the crusade. It seems like the whole event was as much about having good, wholesome fun that is incredibly similar to going to, say, a Limp Bizkit concert, or a hip-hop concert, or a stadium motocross event, or Disneyland (which is just a mile or two from the stadium), but with no drugs or sex—although plenty of rock-and-roll and a nice, wholesome Christian gloss (MOTOCROSS IS THEIR MINISTRY!). And to top it all off, the faithful got to hear a good sermon from a cool-looking, hip pastor who preached a "Bible-based" sermon relevant to the lives of those in attendance. What more could you want on a warm summer evening in southern California?

CONTEXT

Our experiences at the Harvest Crusade, while somewhat more pronounced than what might be experienced at, for example, Greg Laurie's church, Harvest Fellowship (we have never experienced a motocross riding exhibition at any service we've attended), do provide an excellent example of the sort of *appropriation* of popular forms of entertainment and cultural vernacular that churches like Harvest Fellowship and other Christian ministries and organizations provide for their members, attendees, and consumers of the products they're promoting. Indeed, as Greg Laurie has commented, in order to attract people to the Christian message, whether at church or at a crusade, "we have to speak in the language of the culture that we're in."[8]

When confronted with these apparently nontraditional approaches to Christian ministry, most people think of them as being of uniquely current vintage, what with their emphasis on being "relevant" to the current cultural mindset through their use of popular music, theater, art, and various forms of popular entertainment in their efforts to attract both the Christian believer and nonbeliever alike. Yet, as several studies have shown, this has been an emphasis within Christianity at least since the nineteenth century. For example, historian Lawrence Moore (1994) has examined how nineteenth-century Christian ministers who realized that they were suddenly competing in the "marketplace of culture" with other products of mass consumption intended as a means of self-improvement and for personal and perhaps familial leisure, created competing, religious products in response. In this, Moore argues that in their efforts to influence and, in some cases, attempt to ban various commodities intended to make "various forms of leisure and entertainment attractive," religious leaders ultimately ended up creating their own products for sale in the market. According to Moore, "Initially these were restricted to the market for reading material, but their cultural production diversified. Religious leaders even sponsored 'non-profit' organizations with moral and reform goals that competed with the appeal of popular entertainments. By degrees, religion itself took on the shape of a commodity" (1994, 6; for similar accounts, see also Giggie and Winston 2002; McDannell 1998).

Similarly, in her study of nineteenth-century church architecture and Christian worship, Jeanne Halgren Kilde has argued that the way that church buildings were conceived and designed starting in the early decades of the 1800s reoriented evangelical Christianity toward a performance theater model. In this, as Christians began to place greater emphasis on worship as a central component of religious services, as characterized by preaching, responsive readings, hymn singing, and the like, new spaces were developed to accommodate these changes. Thus, Kilde reports that "Choir lofts and soaring organ pipes took up their new locations behind and above pulpit stages, and by the end of the century many churches took on the aura of opera houses, with proscenium arches, marquis lighting, opera boxes, and hinged seats housed within large amphitheatres" (Kilde 2002, 197).

This religion-as-entertainment model, while not comprising the entirety of expressions of Christianity in the nineteenth century, did characterize much of the approach and the way that church spaces were constructed and intended. According to Kilde, congregations competed for the top musicians and orators in their region, were often willing to pay top dollar to retain their services, and often hosted choral and orchestral performances. Further, church buildings were constructed in such a way as to provide the spaces necessary for the variety of activities beyond worship that they offered to believers. Thus, churches began to be organized around attracting a clientele based on what the congregation could offer in preaching, performance, and various programs oriented toward the different members of the family, as compared to what might be available at other competing congregations in any given city (Kilde 2002, 197–200).

Throughout the twentieth century the mass entertainment model expanded to include a much greater variety of parachurch organizations, which often worked in tandem with local congregations, all of which appropriated popular culture and media forms in the service of their mission. For example, beginning as early as the 1930s Irwin Moon, a former pastor who had started his own ministry organization, the intent of which was to combat Darwinism through lectures that utilized various forms of visual media, including a million-volt transformer that he used as his finale, spraying what looked like lightening bolts through his fingertips outward toward the sky, was presenting sermons to thousands of observers at the San Francisco Golden Gate Exposition (Gilbert 1997, 122–26). Moon eventually began utilizing film as a more efficient media through which to bring his message. The films, which typically show Moon using scientific demonstrations to illustrate biblical teaching, can still be purchased today on DVD for home use.[9] Similarly, Billy Graham began his long career as a crusade preacher with his famous 1949

Los Angeles crusade, which was heavily promoted by William Randolph Hearst and his newspapers (see Bagdikian 2000, 42–43), ultimately forming the Billy Graham Evangelistic Association. Among other divisions, the association included a film production and distribution company that both produced and distributed movies for theatrical release as well as distributed films to local church-sponsored events. These movies followed the themes of the day and proved very popular with Christian audiences. One of the early Billy Graham Association movies was *The Restless Ones*, released in 1965 with the tagline "The motion picture that takes you inside the explosive world of today's youth!"[10] Similarly, other youth-themed movies were released in the 1960s. For example, following a few years after the youth gang musical *West Side Story*, a similar Christian-themed movie based on the experiences and a book by David Wilkerson (1966), *The Cross and the Switchblade*, was released, starring Pat Boone and Erik Estrada (later of *CHiPs* fame), and told the story of a small-town pastor ministering to teenage gang members in New York City. Even the fundamentalist Christian school Bob Jones University produced and distributed movies to large church-related audiences. Although their movies were costume dramas involving historical themes with topics as diverse as the Spanish Inquisition and the Civil War in the United States, and not about problematic youth of the 1960s, their appropriation of popular movie productions, despite their opposition to most forms of popular media, illustrates how widespread the appropriation of popular entertainment media had become across a wide range of Christian groups.

Despite the fact that there was a fairly widespread appropriation of various forms of popular entertainment by churches and other Christian ministries, these all operated within the general framework that assumed what might be called a "cultural conversion" that went along with religious conversion. Thus, the angry youth portrayed in the movies, once "saved," no longer looked like gang members or exhibited any sort of counter-cultural self-presentation. The assumption seemed to be that not only did Jesus save people from hell, but also from destructive social or psychological patterns of behavior, and even nonconforming presentations of self, turning them into well-dressed, productive members of the American middle class.

This all changed, however, when Chuck Smith began to open the doors of his then small but growing Calvary Chapel congregation to the local surfers and hippies who were increasingly interested in Christianity (see Miller 1997, especially chapter 2). By accepting these young people as they were, not expecting them to cut their hair or to change out of their jeans and sandals, and, as important (or perhaps more so), encouraging the development of their own expressions of their faith, particularly through their music, Smith and Calvary Chapel transformed conceptions of how Christianity could be expressed. No longer was the only option the stuffy church with the choir, organ, and stained glass sanctuary. This was replaced with what was by comparison a relaxed, casual, come-as-you-are atmosphere that combined with music that echoed the songs being played on popular radio stations—the guitar replacing the organ—initiating a new era in Christian worship and expression in which the church began appropriating the images and symbols of the emerging youth culture.

A particularly important piece of this new expression was how Smith and his staff embraced the music of the younger generation. Not only did the guitar, and eventually entire bands, replace the organ and choirs of their parents' generation, but this music became in many ways the symbolic carrier of this new expression of Christianity. Smith and Calvary Chapel established a record company, Maranatha Music, that produced and distributed a new form of Christian music that was in large part written by the young people attending Calvary Chapel and other similar churches. Their songs were written out of their own experiences, and were, in many ways, indistinguishable in form and rhythm from popular rock or folk music. In the process they exported and popularized a common musical form across the United States and abroad, the results of which are still being felt today (Miller 1997, 83). In this, most anybody could envision themselves playing a guitar and singing these songs, whether at church, in a small Bible study, or just with a few friends at a beach cookout. The extent to which these songs—if not the actual songs, at least songs that are similar in format and sound— are still sung today in churches large and small, liberal and conservative, is a testament to the power of the popular idiom in which their sentiments are expressed. What is important for this discussion is the extent to which popular musical forms were both popularized and democratized such that "everybody" felt ownership of the music, and further, that they were then institutionalized into a distribution network that facilitated the spread of a common experience through a shared musical language across many different types of Christian congregations and denominations.

Just as Chuck Smith and Calvary Chapel popularized soft-rock Christian music and made coming to church in jeans or shorts and sandals acceptable, so the "seeker" churches of the last thirty years have made this approach respectable, and have developed it even further so that now one can have an almost customized church experience, depending on one's taste in music and atmosphere. The seeker movement, pioneered by Bill Hybels and his Willow Creek Church, famously institutionalized their approach through market research as they sought to make church, and the Christian message, "relevant" to the "unchurched" and the "churched" alike (see Sargeant 2000 and Twitchell 2004 for descriptions of Willow Creek and the larger seeker movement). This approach has been both lauded and criticized, and for the same thing. In the words of Kenton Beshore, pastor of the southern California mega church

Mariners Church, "We give them what they want . . . and we give them what they didn't know they wanted—a life change" (quoted in Trueheart 1996). It is important to note that both sides of Beshore's equation are rooted in a consumption ethic. The church provides various religious products, such as music, programs, and good feeling, that people want, and the people leave with that, as well as perhaps a life change, whether that was what they were looking for when they arrived or not. Taken out of context, this sounds a bit like going to the automobile dealership and ending up with a larger, fancier car than what was intended.

In this, the music, theater, and drama, and even the architecture, have been presented by both practitioners and observers alike as "innovative" in their approach to "doing" church. Kimon Howland Sargeant (2000) argues that seeker church leaders "design new, contemporary forms of worship to mirror the musical and cultural preferences of contemporary society. As a result, seeker services are nontraditional and nonliturgical in almost every way. They promote spontaneity and enthusiasm rather than repeating a liturgy continuously. They strive to surprise and intrigue attendees rather than providing worshipers with the familiar and the confessional" (Sargeant 2000, 55). Yet we would argue that this approach isn't really all that innovative; rather, it is really a continuation and further development of the pattern initiated in the nineteenth century in which congregations seek to attract primarily middle-class consumers through their distinctive offerings, providing both a spiritual and consumptive space for everyone in the family.

These efforts are driven primarily by what is popular in the larger culture, or at least in large segments of it—for example, motocross riders for Jesus, T-shirt identities, and music that is virtually indistinguishable from secular pop music (although with Christian lyrics). Even the architecture functions in this way, as it provides the space within which the different services and programs of these churches take place. As Kilde notes, "Though hailed by many as indicating an unprecedented turn in religious architecture, these church complexes are, in fact, firmly rooted in the history of evangelical spaces. From their use of amphitheatre space to their integration of state-of-the-art technology to their rooms and services for every member of the family, these churches carry on the strategies that evangelical churches adopted in the 1870s and 1880s, though they do so in decidedly late twentieth-century language" (Kilde 2002, 215).

In the end, what has developed over time is an increasing emphasis on consumption and personal identity (indeed, often these are indistinguishable) and well being that very effectively mirrors developments in the larger American culture. Cultural forms such as movies, television, and music, as well as lifestyle enclaves, have all been appropriated into a particular stylistic approach to Christianity that aims to make Christianity "relevant" in the cultural marketplace by developing and providing their own cultural products that borrow from, and ultimately appropriate, the dominant cultural forms of expression.

PATTERNS

By "Appropriators," we refer to efforts like those illustrated by the Harvest Crusade, to provide a compelling and "relevant" experience for participants, both those in the audience and those who are performing. In this, both churches and independent ministries seek to create these experiences through imitating or *appropriating* trends found in the larger culture, and ultimately popularizing these through their networks into a particular form of pop-Christianity that is primarily oriented toward creating a compelling individual spiritual experience. Appropriators tend to be situated within the mega/seeker church orbit and ideology, whether actually part of a mega church or not. In fact, in many ways, each of the other three types we have been discussing in this book are at least in part responding to the form of Christianity represented by the mega/seeker model: a bureaucratized and consumption-oriented, franchised form of Christian expression and belief. Thus the mega/seeker church is the primary source of what we describe here, although Appropriators are found beyond those particular locations, and include Christian musical groups, consumer-oriented enterprises sponsored by and at churches as well as at retail stores, and para- church ministries. But it is the desire for relevance and the production of a culturally acceptable product that mirrors the trends in the larger culture in order to attract people to their programs that drives this particular form of Christian expression.

In our visits to different Appropriator churches, concerts, and events, as well as in our examinations of their publications and websites, we have identified one primary pattern, expressed through two main strategies. The primary pattern that charac-terizes Appropriator, and appropriating, activity is that it is all oriented around the individual and her or his personal spiritual experience and identity, whether that be personal salvation, or deliverance from personal problems, or just an enjoyable or moving experience in a worship service or Christian motocross show. In this, individual choice is paramount, such that a dizzy-ing array of options must always be available for the current or potential attendees at these churches or events, which are all, in the end, oriented to serve the personal spiritual, social, and psy-chological needs of the believer, even if these needs are as ephemeral as an entertaining night out with fellow Christians.

This pattern of individual experience/fulfillment/salvation is expressed through two strategies that are rooted in "place": first, the different programs, activities, worship opportunities, and physical spaces are created within the congregation in an effort to provide both a venue for spiritual/psychological wholeness, as well as a social/gathering space within the church compound, and second, efforts are made to create a particular identity and/or experience outside of the church in such different places as the mall, the stadium or arena event, or even through the short-term missions trip, whether in the United States or abroad.

Church as Destination: Programs, Experiences, Activities

The many different programs, experiences, and activities available within the congregation are all organized around providing a personally meaningful place where one can find purpose, healing, salvation, and involvement in any number of different types of ministries, missions trips, or similar projects. This is particularly true for the mega church that has the resources to create and organize programming, experiences, and physical space that the individual can then utilize in her or his own spiritual quest. Several scholars (some more sympathetically than others) have commented on the different characteristics that distinguish the mega church from other churches, such as entertainment space, modeled after the mall and Disney, consumerism, informality, and the like (see Trueheart 1996; Sargeant 2000; Kilde 2002; Twitchell 2004). Most important in this is the way that all of these components are woven together into both an experience and a place for believers to go to find a sense of belonging and community. This echoes what sociologists have called "third places," places that are neither the home nor work, where people can meet and interact with each other in a relatively status-free environment where community building can take place (see Oldenburg 1999).

When we visited several mega churches in southern California, we were struck by how alike each church looked and felt.[11] For example, although Mariners Church in Irvine and Harvest Fellowship in Riverside are located in significantly different communities[12] and have different affiliations (Harvest is part of the Calvary Chapel network, and Mariners is a nondenominational church), both are almost identical in terms of the variety of programs they offer, the way that their physical space is organized, and the way that they are intended to be used by members and visitors alike.

When approaching each church, the first thing one sees is a huge parking area, with the church buildings set well back from the street. At Mariners the parking areas are so large that in the summer of 2006 the church started a shuttle service with large electric golf-type carts to bring churchgoers from their cars parked in the more remote lots. At Harvest, despite the large lots, cars begin lining up thirty minutes before the next service in the hope of securing a space closer to the buildings. If they are unsuccessful, they may have to park in one of the remote lots located a half mile or so away from the church grounds. However, once having arrived at the buildings, partly due to the distance from the busy roadways surrounding the churches, and partly because of the way that the church buildings are laid out, the effect is of being in a separate community from that surrounding the church.

The layouts of the church buildings are themselves very similar. Each church has large public spaces that are intended to be used not only by those attending services on the weekends, but by anyone visiting throughout the week. And why would anyone be visiting the church grounds during the week, one might ask? To shop at the bookstores that rival any Barnes and Noble or Borders store, or to eat lunch at the café that each operates (they serve Starbucks coffee, of course). As a result, the churches are destinations, not unlike the mall, or Starbucks; the grounds are always full of people, whether they are coming to Bible study, or have just dropped their kids off at day care, or are meeting a friend for lunch.

Their worship services and programs are very much alike as well. Each church has excellent music programs and offers engaging, popular music during the worship service. It was interesting to note that the type of music was one difference between the two churches—Harvest maintains an emphasis on guitar- and drum-oriented pop-rock music, while Mariners has now introduced gospel choirs complete with a horn section, and songs that one would more expect to find in an African American church service. This, we found out, is the influence of yet another source—Erwin McManus's Mosaic church in Los Angeles. This regardless of the fact that Mariners is predominantly white, as is their gospel choir, but we see it as another example of the appropriation of what is viewed as successful in other churches and appealing in the larger culture.

Also, in the quest to be relevant, in 2003 Harvest Fellowship began a new worship service on Sunday evenings that it describes as an "innovative Sunday night service for the 21st century."[13] This worship service is specifically marketed to younger people, and includes, as the website describes it, "the latest Christian bands" along with a high-tech, digital feel. The stage is full of video monitors and has an industrial "cool" aura about it, and the speaker for the evening, whether Greg Laurie or one of his associate pastors, utilizes the technology as a way to promote their "relevant" formulation of Christianity. Ultimately, however, the service, just like the Harvest Crusades, centers on the sermon. The "latest Christian bands" and the digital technology are all window dressing for what Harvest really focuses on, the sermon.

As to the programming at Harvest and Mariners, there are of course seemingly hundreds of different programs that one can be involved in, and these are routinely advertised on their websites and in the written materials available at each church, but also in person through different kiosks set up each weekend to let people both see and hear what the different groups are offering to attendees and potential attendees. But most of this is well known, either through media reports or scholarly reports. Churches like these are big places with programs for everybody, and engaging, relevant worship services. And in fact, we saw essentially the same thing at each different mega church we visited, their only limitation being the physical size of their buildings and real estate.

But what we noticed in particular was the emphasis on adaptation to the changing culture and then offering these new (or modified) forms of music, or programs, or venues for worship back to the people in the church. One particular example, experienced at both Mariners and Harvest Fellowship, will illustrate the point. As noted above, both Harvest Fellowship and Mariners operate an upscale café that is intended to be a place for people to meet, talk, relax, etc., and that is modeled after a Starbucks or Seattle's Best, or some other similar restaurant/coffeehouse. Each has ample inside seating areas as well as tables set outside in attractive plazas. Each is decorated in an upscale style that references the larger southern California culture, complete with surfboards hanging from the ceiling and several large-screen plasma video monitors. During the week, these monitors may be showing the latest music videos from Christian bands, or perhaps the past week's worship service, but on the weekends the worship services are shown on these screens. Several observers (e.g., Kilde 2002; Twitchell 2004) have noted the fact that churches like Mariners and Harvest Fellowship have installed these screens in their sanctuaries, but the fact is, these screens are ubiquitous on these campuses. They are not only in the sanctuary, but in the entrance to the sanctuary, in the cafés and in the plazas adjacent to the cafés, and in the bookstores. They are everywhere. During the services, this ensures that the music and message are as ubiquitous around the church campus as the plasma screens (and where there are no video monitors, there are speakers broadcasting the worship service). In fact, this allows people to go to the equivalent of a Starbucks on a Sunday morning and to church, simultaneously.

This is precisely what we observed. At each church we visited, including Harvest Fellowship and Mariners, the cafés were

3-3. Watching the morning worship service from the Global Café, Mariners Church, Irvine, California. Photo by Richard Flory.

completely full; there were no available seats. As the service was beaming into the café (at Mariners' café there are three large plasma screens along a fifty foot wall) people were lining up to order breakfast, while others—families, couples, singles, groups of friends, some reading the newspaper—were eating breakfast, talking with each other, and occasionally looking at the screens. Thus what these churches have created is a space that is a direct appropriation of, and competition for, the otherwise secular café or restaurant, and sacralized it such that it is viewed as an equivalent space to the traditional sanctuary, which for many people is thus no longer necessary. As one person we described this to who had not seen it said, "Now there is a church I could get into!"

Experiences and Activities Outside of Churches

In addition to the many different programs and the new "third spaces" being created within Appropriator churches, there are

also many different efforts to create similar experiences and
gathering spaces outside of the churches in such different venues
as shopping malls, stadium and arena events, and through
"extreme"[14] ministry or missions experiences that are modeled
after so-called extreme sports, such as skateboarding or
motocross, and which often include an international component. What is different is not that these sorts of activities exist—
certainly Christian bookstores, missions trips, and stadium
crusades have been a part of the Christian subculture for many
years. But what is different is the way that these efforts appropriate elements of the larger culture, particularly some of the
more "edgy" developments within youth culture, in the effort
to create and maintain a particular Christian identity or experience for the faithful. These really don't look much different
from any other business or experience, and don't seem to
require much in the way of sacrifice or commitment to any sort
of Christian ideals on the part of their clientele. Instead, they
encourage more of an ethic of consumption—of products and of
experiences.

APPROPRIATING THE MALL. As noted above, one of the models for the mega church has been the mall, with its emphasis on
individual choice and consumer culture as an organizing ideal,
but now elements of the church have gone to the mall itself, as
new "Christian stores" have been established within the last several years. In 2001 Aurelio Barreto, who had made his fortune
with Dogloo, Inc., a company that manufactured doghouses that
looked like Eskimo igloos, sold his company and founded C28,
a Christian retail store that, according to the store website, offers
"an alternative to mainstream mall stores."[15] This is not your
typical Bible bookstore, or even the sort of store that can be
found at most mega churches, as impressive and "cool" as those
may be. These stores have the look and feel of a surf or a skateboard shop, with music and videos playing over the sound

system and on the plasma video screen, and several stylish young people working in the store, all of whom are wearing the clothing sold there. The stores are overflowing with stock—mostly clothing such as T-shirts, sweatshirts, and shorts for men and women, as well as accessories such as earrings, belts, belt buckles, wristbands, hats, and window and bumper stickers for cars. Even a few books and a Bible or two were on the shelves next to the CDs and the DVDs. In fact, from the outside it is very difficult to distinguish a C28 store from any other young adult fashion store in the mall, and really the only way to figure out that C28 is not just another store is to go in, look at the merchandise, and interact with the salespeople.

When we first visited the C28 store in the Main Place Mall in Santa Ana, California, we were met at the door by Troy, a personable young man who had been working for C28 for some time and who was currently splitting his time between a ministry position and managing the Santa Ana store. Troy introduced himself, asked our names—which he remembered throughout our visit—and asked if we had ever been in the store before. When we told him that this was our first visit, he told us that as we looked around we might notice that the store had a "spiritual vibe."

As Troy showed us the different merchandise around the store—we hadn't yet told him that we were not really customers—he took time to explain the different designs on the T-shirts, the jewelry, the belts, the stickers, and everything else, and inquired about whether we had any sort of religious faith. All of this was done in a very friendly manner. We never felt like Troy was trying to convert us; rather, he seemed genuinely excited about the products he was selling, knew all about them, including the stories behind the particular designs, and was both sharing information with us and inquiring about our lives. Both Troy and the other young man working that day were genuinely interested in sharing the story of the store, and their individual

3-4. Car window stickers display at a C28 retail store. Photo by Richard Flory.

faith, but they were also completely oriented toward selling. Troy in fact told us about two young women who had come into the store earlier that day who he said "may have been believers, but obviously weren't living within those beliefs." After he showed them around the store, and explained all the different designs and shared the story of the store, just as he had done with us, they "walked out of here spending $180" on T-shirts for themselves and their husbands.

It is important to note that all of the designs, particularly on the T-shirts and the stickers, are modeled after what is popular in the mainstream surf and skate stores, and look just like what would be found in any surf or skate shop. C28 even carries a least one brand that surf shops carry, "Ezekiel," which was originally founded by Christians but has since been sold. In fact, some of the designers for different products that C28 carries

3-5. A truck in the Harvest Fellowship parking lot with an array of
Christian stickers: Harvest Crusade on the left bumper, Jesus bowing
his head in the middle of the back window, stylized script "Jesus" in the
center of the tailgate, and a Christian fish on the right of the tailgate.
Photo by Richard Flory.

have worked in the surf and skate industry, creating T-shirt
designs for different brands. The difference is that virtually all of
the products in the store have some sort of Christian message
embedded in or on them. As well, C28 has its own brand, "Not
of this World," which includes a complete product line for men
and women and several different sticker designs, which are now
almost as common on southern California roadways as the
Harvest Crusade stickers. The importance of the stickers lies in
their power as a form of consumer identity for those who
emblazon their cars and other personal possessions with certain
logos and designs, and not others. Much of this comes out of the
mainstream surf and skate companies, who use stickers as a sort
of guerilla marketing tactic—suddenly stickers will appear

seemingly everywhere, and if they prove to be successful in appealing to a customer base, then customers begin to put the stickers on their cars, skateboards, and surfboards, ultimately creating a new brand identity, and creating an identity for the customers by associating themselves with that brand. In a similar fashion, C28 has appropriated what might be called the surf/skate "sticker culture" as a way to both advertise the store and to create a Christian identity based on the store logos and slogans.

In a way then, stores like C28 have created both an identity that appeals to Christian young people and in the stores themselves a "third space" of sorts that at once is oriented toward making a profit and promoting a "clean and positive" Christian identity and lifestyle. Barreto sees his stores as places where anyone can come and pray, seek spiritual guidance, and even be converted to Christianity. Barreto and C28 also sponsor events, primarily concerts at malls, with the twin goals of providing a place for Christian young people to gather together and converting some of the people in attendance to the Christian faith as a result of the event and the people they meet and hear speak. Indeed, according to the C28 website, "8,558 people have received eternal salvation, accepted Jesus Christ as Lord and Savior," as a result of the stores and the events that the stores sponsor.[16] But ultimately, as owner Barreto says, the stores have to make money to fund any ministry activities.

MISSIONS AND MINISTRY EVENTS. Just as there are still large stadium-style events such as Harvest Crusade, as we described in the opening to this chapter, so there are many other experience-oriented events as different as professional skateboarder ministries, adventure-themed missions trips abroad, and militant culture wars–oriented youth rallies. These are all organized around the recurring themes that we have seen with the Appropriators: establishing and maintaining a Christian identity, providing an exciting and entertaining experience, and not really requiring much in the way of commitment beyond showing up and enjoying the experience. Some of these experiences are sponsored by Appropriator churches, but most are promoted by independent ministry organizations that range from what appear to be multimillion-dollar enterprises to those that are essentially start-up ministries based on the interests and abilities of the organizers. We have classified these in two categories, "events," in which a group tours to different cities and puts on a show with a particular theme, and "missions," in which a group is organized (either under the auspices of a church, or through a separate missions organization) to participate in a range of activities from evangelism to building houses to providing relief in the wake of a natural disaster.

Regardless the type of activity, each is promoted through a combination of personality and celebrity appeal, focusing on such important considerations as which bands are going to perform, which skaters will be there, or which Christian celebrities might be speaking, and how exciting or entertaining the event or mission will be for everyone who participates. For example, an arena event series that has received some media attention[17] is "Acquire the Fire," intended to simultaneously fight against the efforts of secular media organizations, such as MTV, to attract young people, and to counter it with what they call a "God branding," signifying that one is owned by God and not a secular corporation. These events are framed in very militaristic terms, where young people are encouraged to develop a "battle plan," which can be posted to the Acquire the Fire website on pages that appear to be modeled after MySpace or FaceBook pages, which is exactly the point, to provide an alternative identity for Christian young people that otherwise looks just like what is available in the secular realm. These events have been held in upward of thirty or more cities each year across the United States, with several thousand young people in attendance at each one. Acquire the Fire identifies a particular crisis—that Christian young people are being spirited away from their Christian commitments by "Corporations, media conglomerates, and purveyors of popular culture [that] have spent billions to seduce and enslave our youth." The solution is to create these large-scale events to motivate young people to write their battle plans and thus to fight against the corporations that seek to brand them, and in turn, to get branded by God.

Even missions-oriented activities have lately taken on the "extreme" or adventure emphasis to motivate participants to join a particular missions trip. These trips are organized around what is often referred to as a "short-term mission" in which the participant can use her or his vacation time from work, or summer vacation, or some other limited period of time to experience missions activity. Although one might expect that these sorts of missions activities would be presented as opportunities to serve both others and God, by far the dominant pitch for people to participate is the wonderful experiences they will have and how fulfilled they will feel after participating. Thus, for example, Mariners Church advertises its "Global Outreach" programs as different opportunities that don't take much of a person's time, and presents them as "faith adventures," rather than as missions trips that might demand more of a personal sacrifice. The promotional literature from Mariners reads, "Got a lot going on? We can relate. Fortunately, we have plenty of opportunities for you to serve God without quitting your day job," and says that if a person can share "1 day to 2 weeks of your life on a Faith Adventure trip, you can join God in life transformation and forever change the way you look at the world."[18] Similarly, Go International, an independent missions organization based in Tulsa, Oklahoma, organizes missions trips around the world that sound like they are part adventure, part vacation, and part ministry. The promotional literature for Go

International's summer 2007 Lima, Peru, trip drives the point home:

> Ready for adventure? This year Go International and The Revolution Now[19] are jetting off to Lima, Peru with special guest Ryan Dobson.[20] This is one of those trips you won't want to miss. Picture this: summer time by the Pacific Ocean, Christian rock concert, skate outreach with professional boarders, creative evangelism and friends you'll never forget. You will join with young people from across the country in an adventure of a life time as you take the message of Christ to this amazing land! Using a variety of innovative ministry tools you will help change the lives of thousands of people.

While it is tempting to suggest that the whole mission enterprise, at least as evidenced by these sorts of Appropriator ministries, has been subsumed into the adventure lifestyle perspective, it is clear from reports we have heard and read that good things happen as a result of these efforts. The goals of the trips generally include both evangelistic efforts and service projects, such as helping build or repair housing or sewers, or teaching reading to children or providing health services for a community. As well, the individuals who participate in these missions trips generally find their perspectives on the world significantly broadened, and many participate again in similar missions trips. Whether participants can somehow have it all—enjoy a great adventure, hang out with "professional boarders," meet new friends, *and* find fulfillment in their Christian service is hard to know. Yet it is clear that these ministries, in their efforts to appeal to Christian young people, have appropriated language, symbols, and activities from the larger culture to make these missions trips sound much more like an extreme adventure than a Christian missions trip.

In the end, all of this activity, whether purchasing a Christian-themed T-shirt, hat, or belt buckle, or engaging in the "collective effervescence" of a militant Christian youth rally, or participating in a "skate ministry" in Peru, is about constructing personal identity and having good, clean adventures within a Christian context. And all the accouterments, whether clothing, jewelry, bumper stickers, or music, allow the person to be edgy, or extreme, or cool, but with a nice Christian gloss and identity.

SUMMARY AND CONCLUSIONS

Appropriators, whether within the mega churches or in their own ministry organizations, exhibit an almost uncanny ability to read the larger culture, determine what is most appealing to young people, and then create a new product that successfully appeals to the younger generation of Christians. Yet because of this ability, it is difficult to come to a clear understanding of what Appropriators are actually all about, in large part because they are so amorphous and so prevalent. That is, they are so much like what surrounds them, both in terms of other churches and ministry programs and the larger culture, that it is difficult to determine what is distinct about them. We would argue, however, that this is intentional on the part of Appropriators—their distinctive is that they are largely indistinct from much of the larger culture. Their programs, music, bookstores, cafés, clothing, and the experiences they produce mirror what is available outside of Christian circles, and despite the Christian content, it all ends up looking pretty much like everything else in American popular culture. As a result, it becomes both cool and relatively unobtrusive to be a Christian. In this, Appropriators have created a form of consumer Christianity where one can wear their identity through a T-shirt, bumper sticker, or tattoo, have coffee at their church café, and have what amounts to Christian vacations, all without really giving up any part of an American middle-class consumer lifestyle.

Although many of the Appropriator churches and ministries are framed as being innovative, or "cutting edge," we believe that they are really quite predictable and known quantities. People attend Appropriator churches and events because they know what to expect: a good time, professional-quality entertainment, and that they will feel good about being around and with other Christians. Rather than being innovative or cutting edge, or even new, this is an almost complete embrace of a market/consumer model that requires Appropriators to continually adjust their "product" to the demands of the market, thus reducing the religious demands that can be required of their clientele. There will always be another church or ministry organization that will offer a better program, or experience, or music, and excessive demands just may get in the way of that. Because of their ability to adapt to their market and to appropriate larger cultural currents and give them a Christian gloss, Appropriators will likely be around for quite a while

CHAPTER 4

Resisters

Christians must outthink the world for Christ!

> —Douglas Groothuis, "Outthinking the
> World for Christ: The Mission of Denver
> Seminary's Philosophy of Religion Program"

LA MIRADA, CALIFORNIA

When we heard about the conference that placed two of our types in direct contact with each other, we thought it was too good to be true. We would be able to see how representatives of our Innovators and our Resisters interacted with each other, in particular how they framed what they each saw as the important issues currently facing the church. This was a one-day conference sponsored by Talbot Seminary, and promoted as a "conversation with the emerging church." The brochure listed as "leading the conversation" several faculty members from the school, along with several representatives of the emerging church movement and scholars who had been both studying and working with leaders from the emerging church movement. As listed in the brochure and the online announcement, the goal of the conference was to "partner" with the emerging church movement and to "help them with their theological paradigm." The format was to be driven by several questions, such as, "What does it mean to be an 'Emerging Church'? What is it emerging from and where does it want to go? Is this something we want to participate in?

Are there things we should recognize and embrace? Are there things we should avoid? What honest critique might be helpful?" Clearly this was going to be an eventful and interesting day of dialogue.

Organizing the conference around the idea of a "conversation" meant pairing a representative of the emerging church movement and a Talbot professor, with each addressing the same issue from their particular point of view. The topics included "Setting the Cultural Stage," "Describing the Emerging Church," "Conversations on Community," "Conversations on Worship," "Conversations on Homiletics," and "Conversations on Postmodern Theology/Epistemology." The first set of conversation partners were Robert Webber, a theologian who had written several books that have influenced leaders in the emerging church (see Webber 1999; 2002),[1] and a Talbot philosopher, Garrett DeWeese, who had written a couple of short articles that were highly critical of what he saw as the postmodern tendencies of the emerging church movement.

The "conversation" between Webber and DeWeese set the tone for the rest of the day. Webber spoke first and in story form—in keeping with the Emergent emphasis on narrative and story—using his own life experiences to illustrate his points, talking about various culture changes, most importantly how culture has moved away from propositional/foundationalist knowledge claims, and framing his own personal spiritual journey as an example of moving from a foundationalist epistemology and rationalist theology to a narrative and relational theological perspective. DeWeese, his conversation partner, then proceeded to essentially read from one of the articles he had published three years before (DeWeese 2002), completely ignoring Webber's narrative presentation, while arguing that if the emerging church movement was compared to the 1960s and the Jesus movement—which he had apparently lived through and been involved with—then we've see all this before, there is nothing new in the emerging church, and what might be new is dangerously postmodern.

The rest of the day followed that same pattern. The conference convener would announce each set of speakers, with the introduction of each Talbot speaker including all their academic qualifications, including a listing of their books and articles, thus establishing their academic and theological credentials, and presumably their authority in the conversation. We were constantly being reminded through this ritual introduction that these were the people who were going to "help" the emerging church with their "theological paradigm," which, based on the introductions alone, suggested that they had the authority to critique and to correct the emerging church representatives. Further, just as with Webber and DeWeese, there seemed to be two separate conversations going on during nearly every presentation. First, a Talbot faculty member would get up and read his paper, each of which was an effort to set what he saw as appropriate boundaries for acceptable belief and practice, and then the emerging church representative would get up and essentially say, "Well, that's interesting, but that's not what we do. Here's what we do. We just want to love and serve Jesus," and then proceed to speak out of their different ministry experiences. This aspect of the conversation was not lost on the audience, either. At one point early in the day, during a question-and-answer period following the morning "conversations," one young man stood up, took the microphone, and said, "It seems like there are two different languages being spoken here, you know, like Spanish and Russian, and in some ways they're missing each other." This was a comment to which no one had a response.

Overall, the Talbot faculty members continually referenced the "conversation" in oppositional terms, in that what they were presenting was in effect an effort at setting appropriate boundaries for proper belief, and in opposition to what they believed the emerging church was doing. All of their comments were in the service of their efforts to resist the incursions of developments within Christianity that they saw as harmful. They relied on their academic and theological authority to make their claims, which in general seemed irrelevant to the emerging church representatives. As Spencer Burke, of theooze.com (who was one of the emerging church speakers at the conference), said in response to what he saw as the tendency for boundary setting and categorizing of different perspectives within Christianity, "There is a way in which other people try to define you, and in the modern agenda, because the rules are so important, they say you have to play by these rules. But those rules don't actually exist. We are unpackaging those power and control situations, so that you as modernists are losing more and more of that power and control, to be the, you know, 'spam filter' for theology." For the Talbot presenters, and the type they are representative of, this is one of the main problems with the emerging church and with so-called postmodern approaches to Christianity, that the former structures of authority are being called into question, including what counts for proper belief, and just who is in the proper position to determine what those beliefs are and how they should be believed.

CONTEXT

The oppositional response to developments such as the emerging church, as evidenced in this conference, is a growing trend within certain segments of Christianity. These efforts have primarily originated from men who were largely influenced by evangelical theologian Francis Schaeffer and Campus Crusade for Christ speaker Josh McDowell in the 1970s and 1980s, in particular their evidentiary, legal-rational approach to demonstrating the truth claims of Christianity, and the cultural critique of what they saw as the increasing secularity—usually framed as "secular humanism"—of American society. Through this influence, many of these men went to graduate school, most often in philosophy and/or theology, and then embarked on successful church ministries or academic careers, mostly in Christian colleges and seminaries, although not exclusively.

As a part of their efforts, Resisters have established institutional programs intended to both help in resistance efforts and to train Post-Boomers in their churches and in college and graduate school, and even elementary to high school children, in what they frame as a rational, intellectual Christianity. They have also established networks of like-minded individuals across the United States who participate in each other's conferences, act as guest speakers in churches and in educational settings, publish books together, write articles in each other's publications—both popular and scholarly—and on their websites, and even show up on their own Resister-type radio programs and podcasts, as well as in other, secular media such as local talk radio or television news programs. In each of these activities, Resisters have proven to be incredibly organized and motivated to get their message out through all of these channels, including having a consistent presence in many churches across the United States as guest preachers, and as guest speakers at different church conferences and retreats.

Here we highlight four areas that provide needed context to the rest of the chapter. First, we trace Resisters' lineage as we are able to determine it from their writings; second, we provide a discussion of the institutions and networks they have established; third, we describe how Resisters use various forms of media and how they disseminate their message; and fourth, we describe the general ethos that animates their approach to Christianity and to rival points of view.

Lineage

Although much of the approach to philosophy and theology taken by Resisters, especially their emphasis on rationality and a sort of commonsense realism, appears to be a disembodied, evangelical Protestant appropriation of Thomistic philosophy, this is never acknowledged in any of the Resister writings or in any of the talks or presentations that we heard. Instead, the lineage they detail begins with Josh McDowell (and in many cases Campus Crusade and the "Four Spiritual Laws,"[2] although these are usually left out by name) and Francis Schaeffer and their timely influence in presenting what for Resisters was an intellectually defensible version of Christianity, and moves back through the mid-twentieth-century evangelical theologian Carl F. H. Henry, with some nods to C. S. Lewis and G. K. Chesterton along the way for some international heft, and ultimately invokes the fundamentalist movement of the 1910s and 1920s, usually in the person of J. Gresham Machen.

While Lewis and Chesterton are usually invoked by Resisters, they function more as a way to ground their efforts more broadly in writers many of their followers will recognize, and also apparently to borrow some of their international and intellectual status; it is Henry and Machen who really provide the intellectual capital for the Resisters in their effort to establish a rational, cognitive Christianity. Henry, whose life and career covered most of the twentieth century, was incredibly prolific and influential in his writings, in particular his multi-volume systematic theology, which was used in many seminary programs.[3] Machen was active in the Presbyterian church and a professor of New Testament at Princeton Theological Seminary during the "Fundamentalist-Modernist Controversy" of the 1910s and 1920s. During this time period he wrote *Christianity and Liberalism*, in which he argued that, as signified in the title, modernist Christianity was no longer Christian, but rather a new religion that he called "liberalism." This book in particular is one often cited by Resisters.[4] This construction of a lineage by Resisters, however, leaves out important elements of both Henry and Machen. With Machen, Resisters emphasize his focus on a more intellectual approach to Christianity, and his call to "consecrate" culture to God (Marsden 1980, 137–38), but fail to acknowledge that he broke away from both the Presbyterian church and Princeton Seminary and founded Westminster Seminary and the Orthodox Presbyterian church (Marsden 1980, 192). Thus, the model Machen provides is one of separating from what he saw as unacceptable approaches to the Christian faith, while Resisters intend to resist—ultimately to reform—from within institutions, ultimately hoping to displace old ideologies with their own rational Christian perspective. With Henry, Resisters fail to recognize that as early as 1947 he was criticizing evangelicals for forgetting their social conscience, which, he argued, must be included in any Christian theology; for Henry it was correct doctrine and social responsibility (Henry 1947). Resisters, however, have primarily emphasized a rational, intellectual approach to Christianity and ultimately work toward colonizing American culture and politics with their worldview rather than focusing on the sort of social needs with which Henry was concerned. In the end, owing to the Resisters lineage, their program seems more the logical outcome of Thomas Aquinas, disembodied and filtered through Schaeffer and McDowell, than an allegiance to Machen or Henry.

Institutions and Networks

Resisters have organized many institutions and networks that range from media (both "old" media like radio programs and "new" media like websites and blogs) to educational efforts to well-funded organizations intended to shape public discourse on such seemingly unrelated issues as science (intelligent design) and sexuality, with the aim to mount a challenge to the dominant secular paradigms of American culture. It would be difficult to suggest which of these institutions are more powerful or more important, as the networks that Resisters have developed out of these institutions are what really make their approach successful in attracting followers.

Much of their activity is organized around educational efforts, which include degree programs for seminary students, "great books" programs for undergraduate college students, and what are presented and sold as "Christian worldview training programs" aimed at teenagers. For example, Talbot Seminary in southern California established a master's program in philosophy of religion in the late 1980s with the intention of graduating students who would go on to Ph.D. programs and, ultimately, to careers in the academy, in the process bringing with them a particular philosophical perspective on Christianity. Similarly, Southern Evangelical Seminary, in North Carolina, was founded in 1992 by Norman Geisler for the purpose of developing "competent Christian leadership and service through quality graduate programs" and to provide a "Biblical basis and an academic understanding of our commitment to Christ."[5] These are but two examples. Similar programs exist at seminaries across the United States, in such places as Denver (Denver Seminary) and Fort Lauderdale (Knox Theological Seminary), and scattered Resisters at other schools, such as Gordon Seminary in Boston, Jerry Falwell's Liberty University, Trinity Divinity School in Chicago, Southern Baptist Theological Seminary, and Baylor University, make the rounds as visiting lecturers at various schools and conferences.

What is particularly important about these many different organizations is that those who are involved with one organization are in the same network with others at other organizations, resulting in a much larger network of Resisters than one might imagine. For example, many of the Resisters whose ideas we detail below, while maintaining their particular academic assignments, are also listed as Fellows at the Discovery Institute in Seattle, which, among other things, is the central organization out of which the intelligent design movement is organized. These networks are utilized to publish books together, both multiple authored and edited volumes, to arrange speakers at members' schools and churches, and to organize conferences, with the goal of promoting their particular perspective, especially to young people of college and graduate school age. This is not to suggest that some sort of widespread conspiracy has been developed by Resisters, rather that they have been particularly astute at organizing and utilizing their networks to develop both a coherent message and a strategy for disseminating their message.

One example of the conferences is instructive. In 2003, the first "Love God With All Your Mind Conference" was held in Anaheim, California, with six keynote speakers and several workshop sessions, whose topics included "Making the Case for Christianity," "Nothing but the Truth," "The Resurrection of Jesus and Historical Truth," and "The Redemption of Christianity as a Knowledge Tradition." This conference was specifically oriented toward young people, as conference director Douglas Geivett suggested in the promotional brochure announcing the conference, arguing that because of the "antagonism" that "Christian students face on college campuses from both peers and professors," the conference was "designed to equip college-age Christian thinkers like yourself to articulate their faith in a compelling manner." Geivett assured potential attendees that the conference would include not only opportunities for discussions that would "stretch your mind," but (in an apparent effort to attract the more experientially oriented Post-Boomers and college students) also "dynamic entertainment" and "worshipful music."

The conference itself was held in the shadow of Disneyland and Downtown Disney, the latter being suggested as a good place to go to relax at the close of the conference each day. The "dynamic entertainment" included two performers: a Malcolm Muggeridge impersonator who performed a monologue from Muggeridge over the several days of the conference, in full Muggeridge makeup, and a magician who, the brochure said, had performed at the Hollywood Magic Castle and "for Tom Cruise, Nicole Kidman, DreamWorks, Touchstone, Disney, as well as Steven Spielberg, Pierce Brosnan, and Robert Wise." Dynamic entertainment indeed, which was a bit ironic in that the whole thrust of the conference was to argue for and celebrate a rational, cognitive, and intellectual approach to Christian beliefs, yet the conference organizers opted to use an appeal to "dynamic entertainment," including the proximity to Disneyland and Downtown Disney, in their attempts to attract Post-Boomers to the conference.

In November 2006, a second "With All Your Mind Conference" was held, this time in McLean, Virginia, and for this conference the networks both of speakers and sponsors had expanded considerably. The conference was jointly sponsored by the McLean Bible Church, the C. S. Lewis Institute, the Evangelical Philosophical Society, and the Christian Apologetics Program at Biola University. The speaker roster had expanded from the six keynote speakers, all from the same school for the first conference, to twenty-two speakers from across the United States and abroad.

Thus, the use of their extensive networks allowed the second conference to be much larger and to include a much broader roster of speakers and presenters, suggesting that this trend is expanding within certain segments of Christianity. For example, they included N. T. Wright, a New Testament scholar who has greatly influenced many of the Innovators we detailed in chapter two and, as evidenced both by his writings and by the authors he suggests for "further study," who would not have much in common with the purely cognitive and rationalist Resister framework. What is also interesting, particularly with their inclusion of N. T. Wright, is that this is an instance of a pattern that the Resisters have developed that is actually similar to one used by the Appropriators we detailed in chapter three. That is, the organizers of the second conference not only expanded their speaker rosters, but they included a person, Wright, who is influential among the very groups they oppose, suggesting that they are becoming adept at appropriating representatives, and in some cases language, that they see as attractive to those outside of their networks, in the service of promoting their own program.

Media

Resisters have used several different forms of media to promote their perspective, and have adapted to new media forms as these have become available. As their emphasis has primarily been on the written text and rational argumentation, much of what they believe and wish to promote is published in books, magazines, journals, and the like. Most of this is published through Christian presses, such as Zondervan Publishing and InterVarsity Press, and popular publications, like *Christianity Today*, which makes it readily available in Christian bookstores, Christian college and seminary bookstores, and in church bookstores and libraries. This, in turn, increases their exposure across a broad cross-section of the Christian community.

The ideas in these books and articles are then disseminated through conferences, guest speaking opportunities, such as at conferences and debates sponsored by churches and other organizations, radio, and new media, such as websites, blogs, and podcasts. Websites and blogs publish both original articles from Resisters as well as excerpts and/or adapted selections from Resister books and articles. Blogs also provide reports of different events and public addresses where Resisters have been involved, and comment on current (public) affairs and developments within the church, such as the emerging church, postmodernism, and the like, taking the ideas promoted by the Resister literature and teachings and presenting them in topical popularized versions. In most cases the blogs refer readers back to the original sources, either to the person or event, or to a particular publication of different Resisters, whether book, article, or chapter.

This use of old and new media has expanded the networks that Resisters have established, probably beyond what they could have ever planned. Note as well that these blogs, as with the blogs that appear in any of the types we are describing, all have lists of "friends" or "must read" blogs that are linked, which simultaneously gives an idea of how many other blogs are out there that share this perspective, and thus some indication of the extent of these informal networks that have developed. Some of the potentially more influential websites that Resisters either write for or where their writings are regularly adapted are intended to attract the Post-Boomer generation, complete with innovative-looking graphics and text, and include those owned by such well- known organizations as Focus on the Family[6] and Campus Crusade for Christ.[7] In addition, there are many websites and blogs (many of which also produce podcasts) that are run by individual scholars,[8] laypersons and other commentators,[9] Christian ministries,[10] and Christian publications.[11] Thus, by utilizing the resources of new digital technologies that are heavily trafficked by Post-Boomers, and by making them look and feel like edgy, youth-oriented sites, Resisters are able to promote their perspective to a much wider audience than they would otherwise have been able to do.

Ethos

The overarching ethos that emerges from Resisters is oriented around the idea that Christianity is an embattled minority and under attack in all parts of American culture as well as around the world. In their view, Christianity, or more precisely the "Christian worldview," and traditional morals are under attack by multiculturalists and others who promote relativism in morals and religion. In this, American society was founded on Christian principles but has now become so morally relative that

Christians need to be true to their "absolute" beliefs and "take back" culture in the name of Christ. Much of this is the typical "culture wars" approach popularized by secular pundits such as Rush Limbaugh and Bill O'Reilly, but this is with a particular religious gloss. These views get popularized by such well-known conservative Christian commentators as former Watergate conspirator turned militant evangelical commentator Charles Colson[12] and his former writing partner Nancy Pearcey, and James Dobson, as well as other lesser lights, such as former baseball player Frank Pastore, a local Los Angeles area Christian talk radio host. Colson, for example, recently wrote on his website that liberals are "demonizing religious conservatives" while "Promoting embryo-destructive stem-cell research . . . abortion, special rights for homosexuals, a radical animal-rights agenda, and force-feeding school kids an uncritical view of Darwinian evolution."[13] His former radio show producer and co-author Nancy Pearcey, who recently published *Total Truth: Liberating Christianity From Its Cultural Captivity*, and her husband, Rick, write on their website, "The Pearcey Report," that "America is fighting a two- front war for survival"—one, the war on terror, the other, a culture war between "people who understand that this nation is founded upon the governing principle of independence under God" and those who "reject this founding framework in favor of a concept of independence apart from God." They conclude their column by suggesting that the stakes are cultural survival. If Americans "remember who they are and how they got that way," the odds of survival are increased. Presumably, if Americans forget who they are, either "Islamofascists" or the secularists will destroy American culture.[14] The important aspect of these perspectives is that the solution each provides to the perceived crises facing American culture can only be solved by a return to a what Resisters frame as a Christian worldview, which in their view should be the dominant perspective in American culture.

PATTERNS

By Resisters we refer to those individuals and groups that focus on the recovery of "reason" and are trying to *resist*, or roll back the clock on, postmodern culture, and who want to reestablish the place of the written text and reason as the dominant source for Post-Boomer religious beliefs and practices. In our observations of Resister events, such as public lectures and conferences, and a close reading of their publications[15] we have identified three patterns that characterize Resister efforts: first, developing appropriate rational and cognitive approaches to Christianity; second, opposing postmodernism in the larger culture and in the church; and third, taking over, in their terms "taking back," the culture in the name of Christianity. These should be thought of as interrelated fronts in the continual efforts of the Resisters to identify and resist the various incursions of the larger culture that threaten the integrity of what they understand as historic Christianity. These are both defensive and offensive patterns of response to the perceived threats to Christianity, and are intended to provide resources for believers to defend against bad or improper beliefs in one's personal life, as well as more broadly within the church, and strategies to fight for a particular religious and ideological perspective in the larger culture.

Rational Christianity

Resisters begin with the twin claims that Christianity is rational and that it can be proven that its claims are "objectively true," but also that Christians have abandoned all significant intellectual activity and have become intellectually lazy in their approach to and understanding of their faith, thus reducing Christianity to a private, subjective set of beliefs. Ultimately, their emphasis on the cognitive and rational side of belief is intended to reclaim a perceived lost status for Christian beliefs— if people will take Christians seriously in the intellectual realm (both Christian believers taking their own beliefs as serious intellectual commitments and the larger culture seeing the intellectual value of Christianity), then the lost cultural status of Christianity can be restored.

As the epigraph at the beginning of this chapter suggests, Resisters want Christians to "outthink the world" for a Christian worldview, which starts with their view that Christianity is uniquely rational and therefore objectively true, which, once appropriately understood, can be communicated to the culture intelligently.[16] The idea of reason and rationality, as used by Resisters, tends to shift depending on the context in which they are using it, which is important to keep in mind when reading their writings or listening to one of their lectures. In general however, Resisters argue that reason (and rationality) refers to a property that all humans possess, and that as humans we possess this property because God is rational and logical. Further, reason is the only legitimate avenue for making any knowledge claims or religious faith claims, which are simply another form of rational knowledge. Thus for Resisters, reason forms the foundation upon which all their efforts are based, with all their other efforts growing out of their commitment to reason.

For Resisters, reason, at its most basic definition, means simply that an idea or belief is rational if one has good reason, or "warrant," to believe that it is true. Philosopher J. P. Moreland, writing in his book *Love Your God with All Your Mind*, defines reason as simply using "all our faculties relevant to gaining knowledge and justifying our beliefs about different things." He lists these faculties as the senses, memory, logical abilities, and moral faculty, and continues that using these "in isolation or in combination . . . to gain knowledge and justify my beliefs" demonstrates proper rationality (1997, 43). Further, rationality is not to be considered some static property but an ability one can learn and develop, which Moreland says "should be a high value for the Christian community" (1997, 43). The goal of developing one's reason in relation to her or his beliefs is so that one can reduce the risk of holding false beliefs, and thus be able to rationally calculate the extent to which one holds true rather than false beliefs. Moreland and his colleague William Lane Craig argue that "by learning to be rational and hold beliefs that are justified people trust that they can increase their stock of true beliefs and decrease their number of false ones" (Moreland and Craig 2003, 86; see also Geivett 2005).

Acknowledging the role and importance of reason in relation to one's religious faith is important because faith is not, as most people believe, a "blind act of will, a decision to believe something that is either independent of reason or that is a simple choice to believe while ignoring the paltry lack of evidence for what is believed"; rather, faith should be understood as "*a power or skill to act in accordance with the nature of the kingdom of God*, a trust in what we have reason to believe is true   . Faith is built on reason" (Moreland 1997, 25 [emphasis in original]). Thus, without a "rational foundation" for faith, faith is "unjustified and irrational" (Craig 1994, 17). Further, without a rational foundation for Christian faith, believing in Christianity is just a pragmatic means to selfish ends: "if our allegiance to Christianity is not based on the conviction that it is true and reasonable, then we are treating the faith as a mere means to some self-serving pragmatic end, and that demeans the faith. For example, if we are more concerned with practical application from the Bible than with having good reasons for thinking we have correctly interpreted it, then our bottom line will be that the Bible exists as a tool to make us a success, and we do not exist to place ourselves under what it really says" (Moreland 1997, 99). Thus, Christian believers are encouraged to simply "reaffirm our commitment to truth and right reason" with the confidence that their beliefs "warrant that commitment and will flourish in light of it" (Moreland 1997, 99).

Ultimately, this emphasis on reason and its development in the life of the Christian believer is based on the Resisters' conception of God; since God is "a God of truth, reason, and logic" and humans are made in the image of God, humans embody "the faculty of abstract reasoning and logical thought." Not only that, but owing to this innate capacity, God "invites [his followers] to reason and argue with Him logically, and demands that they present in logical fashion the reason why they believe" (Moreland 1997, 113). Thus, for Resisters, developing an understanding of the rationality of the Christian faith is not an option; not only is the status of one's faith dependent on such an understanding (whether rational or irrational), but God *demands* such a rational, logical faith in his relationship with his followers.

Although these are typical formulations of the role of reason in ascertaining true beliefs and its role in relation to the Christian faith as put forward by various Resisters (see also Geivett 2005; 2006, Groothuis 2000; 2004b; Beckwith 2004), it is a deceptively simple formulation that disguises grander claims for their conception of reason and its role in knowledge in general, and in religious belief in particular, as well as what they seek to accomplish through their emphasis on reason. That is, if the Resister conception of rational faith was restricted to the above, it would be little more than a type of commonsense approach to religious beliefs in which one would be able to construct a logical rationale for one's faith, and then be able to, at least in one's own mind, fulfill the requirements to answer to God in a rational and logical manner as to the reasons for one's belief. Yet Resister claims for reason are much grander than simply having a reason to believe in God and in Christian claims to the truth.

Reason, it turns out, is what legitimates everything related to truth claims in general, and Christianity in particular. According to Resister arguments, rationality legitimates truth. "The claim that a belief is rational means, first and foremost, that we take it to be likely that the belief is true because it *is* rational" (Moreland and Craig 2003, 86 [emphasis in original]). In addition, rationality legitimates biblical revelation: "When we affirm that the Bible is a revelation from God, we do not simply assert that God as a person is known in and through it. We also mean that God has revealed understandable, objectively true propositions. The Lord's Word is not only practically useful, it is also theoretically true (John 17:17)" (Moreland 1997, 45). It is an objectively "true and rational revelation" (Groothuis 2004a, 239), and that "Dividing revelation from logic generates a dangerous and false dichotomy" (Groothuis 2000, 122). Rationality legitimates theological claims: "let us use the term theology to stand for the propositions, theories, and methodologies Christians believe to be rational, true components of historical, biblical Christianity" (Moreland 1993, 8). Rationality also legitimates the activities of the Holy Spirit: "The role of the Holy Spirit is to use our arguments to convince the unbeliever of the truth of Christianity. . . . It is the role of the Holy Spirit to use these arguments . . . to bring people to him" (Craig 1994, 46–48), and, even if Christians aren't aware that their beliefs are rational, they are. "Since beliefs grounded in the objective, veridical witness of the Spirit are part of the deliverances of reason, believers are rational in their faith even if they are bereft of apologetic arguments, as is the case with most Christians today and throughout the history of the church" (Craig 2004, 20).

At root, Resisters believe that reason is universal, that it finds its source in God—"God is a god of truth, reason, and logic"—and is not only inherently present in every individual (although it must, apparently, be learned and developed), but is unchanging over time, and takes the same form in every society and culture. Denver Seminary philosopher Douglas Groothuis frames it this way: "There are essential truths of logic that are necessary for all intelligible thought and rational discourse, Christian or otherwise," and "There are also basic forms of reasoning that are nonnegotiable and are universally valid; they are not matters of contingent social construction or personal taste" (Groothuis 2000, 176–77). In the end, it is this universal rationality that legitimates all truth claims and religious beliefs; such utterances are either congruent with this rationality or they are untrue, or perhaps worse, irrational.

Building on the idea that Christianity is, and must be understood as, fundamentally rational, Resisters then argue for a greater "intellectual" commitment on the part of Christian believers in order to truly understand the essential rationality of their beliefs and to be able to articulate that rationality to themselves and to others. In this, Resisters establish themselves as the authoritative experts who not only point out the deficiencies of the intellectual proclivities of fellow Christians, but who provide the system of understanding Christianity to which Christians should commit. In this, the church is presented as being anti-intellectual, and as having grown lazy intellectually, which has led to a personal/privatized/emotional brand of Christianity that is insufficient for the demands of the world. The solution is to develop an intellectual culture within the church, which will, first, solve the problem of anti-intellectualism in the church; second, create Christians who understand that Christianity is rational and that they need to have rational reasons for their beliefs; third, improve and strengthen the witness of the church and individual believers; and fourth, be both a bulwark against a creeping secularity within Christianity and a defense against an increasingly diverse, pluralistic culture.

In this, Christians are chastised for having lost interest in intellectual activities, and are framed as being "intellectually lazy." Instead of doing the "hard intellectual work" required to understand "God's propositional revelation," they rely on private experiences and emotions for their knowledge and understanding of the Christian faith. Moreland traces this

development to the Great Awakenings of the nineteenth century and the personalistic pietism that followed, resulting in, as
he describes it, a religion of "subjective feelings, sincere motives,
personal piety, and blind faith" (1997, 26–27). The result, he
says, is that "modern Christians are largely illiterate about the
content of their own religion and feel inadequate because of
it. . . . We must develop intelligent Christians; that is, Christians
who have the mental training to see issues clearly, make important distinctions carefully, and weigh various factors appropriately" (1997, 48). Intellectual engagement with Christianity,
developing one's mental and cognitive abilities, is, he believes,
ultimately a fundamental component of one's Christian calling,
and should be a part of one's service to God: "Among other
things, we are to love the Lord our God with all our minds
(Matt. 22:37), we are to destroy speculations and every lofty
thing raised up against the knowledge of God and take every
thought captive to Christ (2 Cor. 10:5), and we are to give
everyone a reason for the hope that is within us (1 Pet. 3:15). In
short, our desire to serve and honor Christ implies (and presup-
poses) a desire to know and do the truth, and this implies a need
to cultivate our cognitive faculties as part of our service"
(Moreland 1993, 8).

William Lane Craig expresses similar sentiments, and argues
that intellectual activity is essential, not only for "Christian
scholars and pastors . . . [but] Christian laymen, too need to
become intellectually engaged. Our churches are filled with
Christians who are idling in intellectual neutral. As Christians,
their minds are going to waste. One result of this is an immature,
superficial faith. People who simply ride the roller coaster of
emotional experience are cheating themselves out of a deeper
and richer Christian faith by neglecting the intellectual side of
that faith" (1994, xiv). The result of this "intellectual idling" is
that everyday Christians "know little of the riches of deep
understanding of Christian truth, of the confidence inspired by

the discovery that one's faith is logical and fits the facts of experience, of the stability brought to one's life by the conviction that one's faith is objectively true" (1994, xiv).

Resisters further suggest that not only is Christianity rational, and that Christians need to develop their rational capacities and thus become more intelligent in their Christian faith, but that Christianity can even be considered as a scientific enterprise. As former UC Berkeley law professor, and self-professed father of the intelligent design movement and the originator of the so-called Wedge Strategy,[17] Phillip Johnson has said in regard to Christian beliefs that "we are taking an intuition most people have and making it a scientific and academic enterprise."[18] Similarly, J. P. Moreland, in the introduction to an edited volume that was the outcome of an intelligent design conference in the mid-1990s, has argued for "theistic science," going beyond the typical argument for an intelligent designer as the originator of the universe to arguing that the "inference to God justified by [design arguments] can be seen as, in part *scientific* matters. True, the most important issue is whether the inference to God is a rational one, not whether it is an issue of science. Theology does not need the support of science to be rational. But given the general respect of science in our culture, it is still interesting to consider the relative merits of theistic science . . . and evolutionary theory as rival *scientific* hypotheses" (Moreland 1994, 33 [emphasis in original]). Thus, in this view, although again reason and rationality are the most important elements, the existence of God is considered a scientific possibility, thus rendering even God as being subject to the authority of reason, and perhaps even science.

Against Postmodernism

In addition to attempting to set out an argument for a rational, cognitive form of Christianity, Resisters have made a significant effort to oppose, or resist, the influences of postmodernism in both the larger culture and particularly the Christian church, where in their view it has made inroads through theologians, ministers, and laypersons. These "postmodern" Christians are framed by Resisters as either naive and unaware of the dangers associated with postmodern thinking, or as individuals who are well aware of what postmodern thinking means for Christianity, and thus are actively seeking to change two thousand years of Christian orthodoxy. We focus particularly on their resistance to the inroads of postmodernism in the life and ministry of the church, in particular as directed at the "emerging church" movement.[19] It is important to note here that the term "postmodernism" as used by Resisters is in many ways shorthand for all those things that Resisters are opposed to, including the increasingly pluralistic American culture. It is essentially a residual category into which all perceived threats to a rational and objective Christianity, and their own moral systems, can be placed—in particular, that which threatens their perception of appropriate, traditional authority structures.[20]

According to Resisters, postmodernism rejects objective reality (and truth) for a culturally relative "anything goes" perspectivalism; foundationalist epistemology for knowledge legitimated in and through community; metanarratives for micronarratives; and propositional knowledge (and truth) for story and narrative. These substitutions then necessarily lead to a pluralism and relativism where no one set of truth claims have any greater status relative to the truth than any other set of truth claims. This is usually framed in extremely individualistic and moralistic terms—"what is true for you is not necessarily true for me"—that begin with religious claims and are ultimately related to social-moral concerns such as sex and sexuality, abortion, euthanasia, and family issues. Resisters frame this in what amounts to a formula for correct moral behavior by arguing that in order to act correctly/morally, one must first think correctly—which for Resisters would entail having the appropriately rational basis for one's Christian beliefs. According to Resisters, right actions cannot possibly follow from believing wrongly. For Resisters then, postmodernism challenges the very basis of their religious enterprise, since as they interpret it, postmodernism denies the accessibility of absolute, universal, objective truth by way of reason that is equally accessible to all people in all places and in all historical time periods.

Owing to their understanding of Christianity as uniquely rational and logical, and postmodernism as fundamentally irrational, it is fairly easy to see how Resisters have mounted a vociferous resistance to what they see as the inroads that postmodernism has been making into Christian thought and practice. This effort originates primarily with conservative, rationalist Christian philosophers and biblical scholars in books published by Christian publishing houses, but also through magazine columns, popular lectures and sermons, talk radio shows, websites and webzines, blogs, and podcasts. As noted, this effort is particularly aimed at the "emerging church" movement, both its leaders and practitioners, and although some of the critique is presented in a manner intended to be constructive and qualifiedly supportive of some of the emerging church efforts, most of it is presented in an overtly authoritarian, condescending, and combative manner, suggesting that there may be something else at stake for Resisters than just religious beliefs as they face the challenge of postmodernism. We will return to this theme in the conclusion, as we raise questions about the claims that the Resisters make.

Some of the Resister opposition to postmodernism, and to the emerging church movement in particular, frames these developments as being a stylistic protest movement of sorts, not unlike what any adolescent goes through with her or his parents, protesting and rebelling against the authority and shortcomings of the very traditions out of which they are "emerging." For example, New Testament scholar D. A. Carson (2005) argues that the "whiff of protest in the emerging church movement is everywhere," and identifies three fronts of protest. First, he says, they are protesting their received religious heritage and its "personally stifling cultural conservatism"; second, they are protesting the epistemological certainties of modernism, particularly its "incarnation in modern churchmanship"; and third, they are protesting "modernism's incarnation" in the seeker-sensitive/mega church model of Christianity, in particular the impersonal nature of their marketing techniques and bureaucratic organizational form (2005, 41). Similarly, philosopher Garrett DeWeese suggests that there is nothing new to see in the emerging church or in emerging culture, arguing that the "whole emergent movement will be seen a decade from now to have been simply the fad du jour, an irritating distraction at best, a disillusioning waste of time and effort at worst. . . . There is nothing important, or new, or even very interesting about postmodern emerging culture" (DeWeese 2005, 424). He agrees with Carson's assessment of its protest character by suggesting that it is just marketing itself to "a predominately young segment of society who, like young people everywhere and always, need to rebel against authority and tradition, believing themselves to be the first ever to discover the truth" (DeWeese 2005, 425).

More significantly, however, Resisters oppose what they see as the rejection of reason as a way to access objective and absolute truth. Indeed, they understand the emerging church as rejecting objective truth by assuming a postmodern worldview and its relativistic- and narrative-based understanding of truth. Philosopher Douglas Groothuis argues that postmodernism, as being imported into Christianity through the popular publications of such emerging church leaders as Brian McLaren and others, several of whom we have identified in this book as Innovators, is specifically and intentionally undermining an emphasis on rational, objective truth in Christian belief.

In response to this postmodern emphasis within Christianity, Groothuis argues that historically "defenders of the Christian worldview have argued that the biblical worldview is both objectively true and rational (Is 1:18; 1 Pet 3:15; Jude 3). It is derived from the Bible, which contains a true and rational revelation" (2004, 239), whereas postmodernism rejects the Christian claim to be "true, rational and knowable" because it "rejects notions of absolute truth and binding rationality . . . as well as the notion that language can unambiguously communicate matters of ultimate meaning," and replaces them with a conception of truth that is "a matter of perspective only; it is something that individuals and communities construct primarily through language" (2004, 239–40). He concludes that if this view of truth is accepted, "objective truth is ruled out in principle. Truth dissolves into communities, ethnic groups, genders, power relationships and other contingent factors. No one meta-narrative (or worldview) can rightly claim to be a true and rational account of reality" (2004, 240).

Philosopher R. Douglas Geivett sounds a similar warning in his critique of the "narrative turn" in postmodern theology. In this, Geivett distinguishes between "story" and "account," suggesting that the former can only mean "make-believe," where one suspends belief and "we play a role *as if* we believed" (2005, 38 [emphasis in original]), and is thus inadequate as a basis for rational, evidentiary-based Christian theology. Geivett instead calls for Christians to be accountants of sorts, in which believers need to continually be taking account of the available evidence so as to determine whether their beliefs are really true, thus reducing their risk of having false beliefs. In this way, individuals (who are, according to Geivett, "by nature evidence-gatherers" [2006, 7]) fulfill one of their most basic anthropological drives, to gather the evidence necessary to come to true and rational beliefs. An appropriately accurate account—that is, one that matches the gathered evidence—says

Geivett, compels belief, whereas a story "simply invites imaginative participation" in the narrative (2005, 39), which he has already determined is just make-believe, and thus cannot encompass the rational, absolute truth of Christianity.

The outcome, as argued by Resisters, is that Christians who are embracing a postmodern approach in their individual lives and in their churches are not sufficiently biblical in their efforts (Carson 2005, 87; Erickson 2004, 342), have "rejected logical consistency as a criterion for theology" (Groothuis 2000, 120), have given up objective, absolute, and propositional truth (Groothuis 2004a; 2004b) for a subjective truth realized through personal experience (Geivett 2005) and a trendy, "hip," and currently stylish theological belief system that challenges traditional notions of authority in the church (Geivett 2006; DeWeese 2005).

The issue of traditional ideas of authority in the church is one that seems to permeate the entire Resister opposition to postmodernism and to its influence in the Christian church. The language used throughout the Resister arguments seems intended to establish an expert system that functions as a defense for their particular understanding of Christianity, which is always framed as "historical," or "orthodox," and with the Resisters themselves as the credentialed philosophers and theologians able to determine this, and thus, the authoritative arbiters of the only appropriate approach to Christian theology and belief. In one of the more blunt formulations, these issues of authority are laid out in precise terms. Southern Baptist Seminary theologian Chad Owen Brand, writing in the edited volume *Reclaiming the Center: Confronting Evangelical Accommodation in Postmodern Times* (even the title suggests this very issue of authority), argues that postmodern theologians and ministers are "employing a democratic set of ideologies and methodologies for doing theological construction" and in those efforts are "in danger of seeking the 'Spirit's guidance' in an uncontrolled epistemological environment" (Brand 2004, 304). The issue then seems to be one of who actually has authority and control over epistemology and the interpretation of Christian history; theology and tradition and, for Brand at least, even the Spirit cannot be given free rein in an "uncontrolled epistemological environment" lest authority be transferred to an uncontrollable, unpredictable, and irrational entity.

Making American Culture Christian

Even as Resisters promote Christianity as uniquely rational, and alternately chastise Christians about their lack of intellectual basis for their faith because of the self-serving pragmatic ends that this promotes, and encourage them to become more "intellectual" by becoming more rational (Moreland 1997), it turns out that in the end their arguments for the rationality of Christianity are entirely pragmatic in nature. Moreland and Craig (2003, 2), for example, make the argument that since the university is the "single most important institution shaping Western culture, [if] the Christian worldview can be restored to a place of prominence and respect at the university, it will have a leavening effect throughout society. If we change the university, we change our culture through those who shape culture." This pragmatic, cause-and-effect approach can be found in one way or another in most forms of the Resister pronouncements and institutions, the goal being to establish the rationality of Christianity not only as important for the spiritual lives of Christian believers, but so as to make Christianity somehow respectable in the larger culture, and ultimately to restore the "Christian worldview" to its rightful, authoritative place in American culture.

Given that on the one hand Resisters argue that American culture is completely relativistic, pluralistic, and postmodern, and has rejected reason and any propositional arguments for truth and the existence of God, while simultaneously arguing that American culture can be taken over and a Christian world-view established as the authoritative perspective if it can be shown to be intellectually viable through demonstrating that Christianity and a Christian worldview are rational, this argument seems to work at cross purposes with their diagnosis of American culture. Be that as it may, the arguments from Resister philosophers, biblical scholars, and theologians for establishing the Christian worldview as dominant in American culture are, as we discussed above, disseminated through various channels to a wider Christian audience through such popular media as Christian books and magazines, educational programs aimed at students from elementary school through seminary-type training, radio, and new media, such as websites, blogs, and podcasts.

The general pattern in this is to capitalize on a preexisting concern or fear among Christian believers, most often having to do with personal and social-moral issues, and in particular a concern for their children and the cultural environment in which they are growing up, and then to suggest those persons, worldviews, perspectives, etc., that are responsible for the bad state of affairs. Most of this is typical culture wars positioning—straw man arguments about the "enemy," and then explanations of how a Christian worldview is superior to any other worldview, particularly in terms of its rational consistency and the kinds of behavior and moral actions that Resisters expect will follow from proper beliefs (Geivett 2005, 46–47; Moreland 1997, 73). This is ultimately where all the Resisters end up, that American culture has embraced naturalism, scientific and otherwise, which has led to the irrational cultural mindset of postmodernism, leading to relativism, cultural chaos, and an anything goes morality. For Resisters, the only way out of this is to "reclaim" the culture for Christianity and Christian values and the Christian "worldview," a broadly defined perspective that is centered on a personal moral system that upholds chastity, fidelity, heterosexuality, and the bio-nuclear family values that argue against homosexuality and abortion, and which promotes the "proper" forms of authority, both secular and religious. This then functions as a rallying point for followers who might not otherwise be too interested in the rationalist perspective that Resisters promote, but who are interested in somehow stemming what they see as the moral decay of the American culture.

As noted previously, this perspective finds its way into the everyday life of Christian believers in a variety of ways, through a variety of spokespersons, both famous and not-so-famous, whether Charles Colson or James Dobson, or local Christian talk radio shows hosted by self-styled intellectual defenders of the Christian worldview, or through websites or blogs. These more popular efforts find their source in many of the Resisters we have been highlighting here, primarily due to their ability to get their books, recordings, columns, papers, etc., disseminated through the various networks and media forms in which they are active.

The groundwork is laid for this pattern by Resisters, who argue that because conservative Christians withdrew from public and intellectual life in the late nineteenth and early twentieth centuries, opting instead for a personal pietism in their faith, America has become secularized and inhospitable to Christians and the Christian worldview. In this, not only is America a secular, pluralist, and morally relativist culture, but Christians and their views are under attack, despite the tolerance in culture for other religious, cultural, and lifestyle perspectives. In this, Resisters call for establishing a reason-based Christian worldview as the only way to restore that worldview as the dominant and pervasive worldview in American culture. This ultimately, according to Resisters, will result in the proper type of society with the proper type of morals and beliefs.

At one level, this is connected to the Resister emphasis that "right behavior" can only follow from right thinking and belief. As we hear repeatedly from Resisters, "belief is the engine that drives behavior. The best way to cure wrong action is to identify wrong beliefs" (Geivett 2006, 7). Yet at another level, it is about elevating "rational Christianity" to a competitive level in the "marketplace of ideas," with the goal of having "the Christian worldview" dominant in culture, which would then determine the kinds of laws, families, and even science that is appropriate in American culture.

Two examples from a single volume of arguments for the intelligent design movement demonstrate this pattern.[21] Although most of the controversy surrounding the intelligent design versus Darwinism movement is focused on its scientific aspects, there is behind it a much different goal than simply teaching intelligent design as an alternative scientific perspective, or of even getting religion—particularly conservative Christianity—into the classroom. Getting a hearing for intelligent design is essentially the "thin edge of the wedge strategy," which is intended to open the way to restoring a Christian worldview to its rightful authoritative place in culture (see Johnson 1995; 2000). For example, Nancy Pearcey writes that "most people sense instinctively that there is much more at stake here than a scientific theory— that a link exists between the material order and the moral order. . . . The question of our origin determines our destiny. . . . Our view of origins shapes our understanding of ethics, law, education—and yes, even sexuality" (Pearcey 2001, 45). She continues that the public, presumably including that portion that other Resisters have framed as being not intellectually inclined, are "intensely interested in what Darwinism means for a general worldview" and concludes that what is "at stake in this controversy is which worldview will permeate and shape our culture. . . . And because Darwinian naturalists use all their cultural power to undercut design at every turn, today we're going to have to learn how to explain these worldview issues even to our toddlers" (Pearcey 2001, 50).

In the same volume, John G. West Jr., a political scientist at Seattle Pacific University, and a senior fellow and associate director of the Center for Science and Culture at the Discovery Institute in Seattle, argues for a simple causal structure in which scientific materialism is the sole cause of all the ills of American society, and claims that intelligent design, if only it can become dominant in science, and by extension in schools and throughout society, is the cure for all the problems caused by scientific materialism (West 2001). West provides a long list of ills caused by scientific materialism, which sound as much like a conservative political ideology as they do a cultural critique. In this, scientific materialism has "spawned the twin legacies of social Darwinism and socialism," helped create the modern welfare state, undermined the belief in the "ability of the poor to surmount their material conditions," "undermined theories of personal responsibility" in the criminal justice system, led to a decrease in imprisonment "even for violent offenders," decriminalized "such behaviors as public drunkenness," "reshaped the field of medicine" resulting in a "vigorous eugenics movement," eroded "traditional beliefs about family life and marriage," narrowed the "acceptable range of debate in the natural and social sciences," brought about "extreme forms of multiculturalism and feminism," and even brought about postmodernism (West 2001, 62–65).

For West, the solution—which again is a single variable that alone can reverse all the damage that scientific materialism has caused—is to get scientists to "change fundamentally how they view man and the universe," (2001, 65) moving to a view that favors an intelligent designer, which will then have what he sees as essentially the opposite "trickle down" effects on society and culture. Thus, if intelligent design (and its assumptions) become the dominant scientific paradigm, "the case for free will and personal responsibility" will be reinvigorated, in social welfare policy "issues of character and accountability" will replace the goal of alleviating material needs such as food and shelter, it will provide a "powerful way to check the moral relativism spawned by scientific materialism, especially in the area of family life and sexual behavior," it will "expand the context in which issues such as abortion and euthanasia are debated," it will provide a "defense of science itself . . . [removing] one of the chief inspirations for the postmodern impulse and helping restore the integrity of science," and finally, it will support and be more consistent with "free inquiry" and "unhindered scientific exploration" because, unlike scientific materialism, "intelligent design is not monocausal" (2001, 65–68).

These are not isolated examples. This perspective can be found in such seemingly unrelated sources as undergraduate college programs and talk radio shows. John Mark Reynolds, who directs an undergraduate program at Biola University in southern California that, according to him, has been called the "educational arm of the wedge strategy," and one that intelligent design guru Phillip Johnson regularly shills for (see Johnson 2007), says that his program is "at war with the modern culture. [We] do not want to 'get along' with materialism, secularism, naturalism, post-modernism, radical feminism, or spiritualism."[22] In fact, from Reynolds's perspective "history is going the wrong way. Yuk. We are reactionaries and proud of it."[23] Frank Pastore, a former Major League Baseball pitcher[24] and host of his own Los Angeles Christian drive time talk radio show, billed as "the intersection of faith and reason," has expressed a similar perspective. In a *Los Angeles Times* editorial published just after the 2004 general election, Pastore argued that the American voters had "rejected liberalism, primarily because liberalism has been taken captive by the left" and that the left must be "defeated in the realm of ideas" because it "vomits upon the morals, values and traditions we hold sacred: God, family and country." The defeat of the left and the rejection of its values, Pastore claimed, ensures that America will continue to be "that shining city set on a hill" (Pastore 2004). For Pastore, the only nation that can save the world from "secular communism, European socialism, and the Islamo- fascist threat" is a Christian America (Trammel 2007).

Thus, for Resisters the emphases on reason, developing one's mind, cultivating the "Christian worldview," and defeating liberals who denigrate core American values are, in the end, oriented toward a new version of postmillennialism, where rational Christianity is the dominant ideology that will usher in the (presumably rational) kingdom of God—which will apparently be located in the United States.

SUMMARY AND CONCLUSIONS

As we conclude this chapter, it is important to point out what should be obvious—that there are other traditions within Christianity that could also be framed as "resisting" various elements of American culture, that, for example, emphasize social justice in contrast to consumer culture, such as that promoted by Jim Wallis (see Wallis 2005a; 2005b), or who provide a critique, such as that of Stanley Hauerwas, of what might be called Christian nationalism (see for example Hauerwas 1991; 2000). But these forms of "resistance" (and we're not suggesting that these people consider themselves "resisters" in the sense we are using the term) are against forms of cultural accommodation by Christians that the Resisters as we have described them here accept both as good and as indicators of the Christian origins of America. That is, in the end, the rationalist Christian worldview is one of extreme individualism, traditional authority, and a conservative political ideology that is glossed with claims to Christian values. The efforts of the Resisters we have profiled here are commanding attention in various ways, whether through their efforts at the local church level, in educational institutions, or in some cases in the larger political and cultural sphere.

Our Resisters are intent on resisting a changing social and cultural order where their conception of reason and rationality is under attack, or more accurately (at least according to their analysis) completely disregarded, and are trying mightily to regain a voice for a commitment to reason and rationalism that legitimates everything they believe in and, they argue, legitimates everything anybody should believe in. Further, not content to limit their efforts to the personal religious sphere, they want a rationally ordered world, and propose to "reestablish" what they call a "Christian worldview" as the dominant ideology in American society and culture.

The institutions and networks they have developed allow their message to be disseminated through a variety of media, from academic to religious to popular culture, through schools and training institutes, radio programs, websites, and blogs, and they are connected to powerful and heavily funded political players like the Discovery Institute, and James Dobson and others, as well as to venerable conservative Christian groups like Campus Crusade and their many and varied presences in real and virtual life.

From our analysis, we raise four issues that in turn help us to understand the Resisters in contrast to the other approaches to Christianity we are describing in this book. First, whether sitting through a lecture, sermon, or other presentation by Resisters, or reading one of their books, articles, or reviews, one is struck by a certain attitude that permeates their presentation. Although they consistently claim that their aim is to be "winsome" representatives of Christianity, their defensive, authoritarian, aggressive, and often condescending critique of any rival perspective suggests that there is another set of concerns for Resisters than just obtaining a voice for Christianity in the larger culture. A short list of these other concerns would include a perceived loss of cultural authority for their perspective—and perhaps as importantly, for them personally—to younger people,

women, and different race or class or ethnic or cultural understandings of Christianity. In this they have set up what is essentially an expert system in which they alone are able to determine
what is or isn't "rational" and thus true, and which in the
process devalues other perspectives as being somehow illogical,
irrational, or otherwise inferior belief systems.

Some examples of Resisters who display this aggressive and
condescending attitude and approach include D. A. Carson,
who sees the emerging church movement as having the "whiff
of protest . . . everywhere" (2005, 41) and suggests that it
needs to "spend more time in careful study of Scripture and
theology . . . even if that takes away some of the hours they have
devoted to trying to understand the culture in which they find
themselves" (2005, 234). For Carson, the emerging churches are
"self-indulgent" and filled with "disgruntled conservatives," and
he suggests that the emerging church's emphasis on authenticity
is "slightly smarmy."[25] Carson further characterizes an influential book by theologian Stanley Grenz as "a disappointment. . . .
It has the flavor of the amateurish about it" (2004, 54). Other
examples include Douglas Groothuis on the "correspondence
theory of truth," in a chapter he published in a book that in its
introduction explicitly claims to be an academic book, but suggests that "it can become a bit technical in some of its details"
(2004b, 79), apparently even for the academics for whom the
book is intended. Similarly, Douglas Geivett claims that "most
English-users have never seen [the word epistemology] before,
or heard it pronounced," concluding, "'Tis a pity" (2005, 40),
and then proceeds to reinforce that it is an area for philosophers
only, who alone can then inform the layperson as to good or bad
epistemological methods. Garrett DeWeese is just grumpy about
postmodernism and those who would try to claim it in some
form for Christianity. According to DeWeese, "Emerging culture is simply narcissistic individualism riding the momentum
of consumerism" and "the emerging church movement simply

offers niche marketing" (2005, 425), and he follows these claims up with, "I am annoyed by those who proclaim that the church must be relevant to postmodern culture" (2005, 426). Thus despite their claims to their being "winsome ambassadors for Christ,"[26] they evidence a lack of grace and a generally unpleasant perspective that is hostile to all other viewpoints that might challenge their efforts.

Second, the more we listened to and read material from Resisters, it became clear that their use of "reason" ends up being a sort of "we believe this is true because its rational, and it is rational because it is true" circular argument based on a priori assumptions of truth and reality, which aren't necessarily "objective" (in the sense that "everyone" can see them to be true) unless one shares those same assumptions. This strategy is ultimately linked to their claim that reason is universal, originates in God, and is available to everyone in all historical periods and in all cultures in exactly the same way. Yet this view of reason seems difficult to maintain in the face of both empirical evidence and social theoretical and philosophical arguments that demonstrate that there are multiple logics and rationalities that operate in the empirical and the philosophical world that are capable of representing "truth." For example, anthropologist and philosopher of science Helen Verran's study of Nigerian mathematical systems shows that not only are logic and math culturally relative, but that numerical quantities in the Nigerian system are in fact not absolute but always relational. In other words, contrary to one example that Resisters commonly use and to what might make "common sense" in American culture, one plus one does not always equal two, as there may be differing conceptions of the units involved and their relationship to each other. Thus, even though Resisters argue for a universal reason and logic, the case of Nigerian mathematics provides at least one counter case to their assumptions, since that system is based on social practice rather than abstract logic (see Verran

2001). Philosopher Walter Watson, building on the ideas of Richard McKeon, has argued that one of the most significant philosophic discoveries of the twentieth century was the "fact of pluralism, that the truth admits of more than one valid formulation" and that this is "inseparable from the nature of thought itself" (1985, ix), suggesting that the one way to truth that Resisters argue for is simply nonexistent. Indeed, as sociologist Christian Smith has argued, "The strong foundationalism that underwrote a supposedly universal rationality that definitely adjudicated between human differences is dead" (Christian Smith 2003, 92).

Third, the Resisters' critique of the anti-intellectualism they see in Christianity is fairly limited in scope, and seems to be primarily oriented toward the mass-Christianity/seeker movement–informed segments of Christianity in which "felt needs" and personal experience are driving the teaching and activities of the church—at least according to Resisters—usually at the expense of developing greater cognitive knowledge of the rational approach to Christianity that Resisters claim and promote. But their claim of anti-intellectualism in the church seems not to match their resistance and opposition to the emerging church and postmodernism. For example, it could be argued that the emerging church movement is largely the result of intellectually active, thoughtful ministers and laypersons alike (setting aside whatever one thinks of their position), as evidenced at least by the more well-known leaders and ministers, all of whom have college and in many cases seminary and graduate school educations. Despite this, much of the Resister critique of their effort is couched in terms such as "amateurish" and suggests that those involved in the emerging church movement are unwitting as to the real meaning of postmodernism and its perceived threat to reason and logic.

What seems more likely is that whether for religious or for cultural authority reasons, Resisters oppose these developments not because of their lack of intellectual grounding, but for the threat they pose to Resister understanding of and position within particular segments of Christianity, as well as what they see as a proper epistemological grounding for personal and social morals and behavior. Clearly they feel their position is threatened by postmodernism in general and particularly as it makes its way into the church. Just as clearly, they believe that in order for one to behave or act in morally appropriate ways, one must first have the proper set of epistemological assumptions and beliefs—otherwise, it's everyone for themselves, moral and social chaos. Yet, as Resisters themselves claim, one's most basic beliefs are revealed through action, thus it is at least plausible that if people act in ways that are congruent with biblical teaching—which, for example, our Innovators strive to do, despite their reliance on some postmodern ideas—that would imply "correct" beliefs, whether they understand their faith in postmodern or in rationalist terms.

Finally, in their critiques of postmodernism, Resisters present nearly identical caricatures of postmodernism, based on what appear to be readings of secondary sources, usually summarized by other Resisters, rather than readings of the original sources of postmodernism.[27] For example, the typical Resister critique of postmodernism starts out with Jean François Lyotard's statement defining postmodernism "as incredulity toward metanarratives" (Lyotard 1984, xxiv) and then claims that this means worldviews, such as their own conception of Christianity, and thus by extension Christianity as a worldview, are not viable from a postmodern perspective. But as Calvin College philosopher James K. A. Smith (2005) has pointed out, not only is this an incorrect reading of Lyotard, but a correct reading of Lyotard is actually much more friendly toward what most Christians would believe about the truth claims of Christianity. That is, Lyotard's discussion of "metanarrative" relates to the *legitimation* of truth claims, not the *scope* of the claims that are made. Thus,

Lyotard argues that knowledge of all sorts can no longer be legitimated by referring to a universal reason such as that characterized by modernity, but that even science must resort to some sort of legitimating myth, which places beliefs back in the realm of faith, and not reason and/or science. Christian Smith argues in a similar vein that it is narratives that provide the very essence of who we are as humans who are "moral, believing animals," not some form of foundationalist epistemology or reason that tells us who we are. Note that Smith is not advocating a "postmodern" perspective here, but is arguing first that narratives are essential to who we are as humans, and second, that rationally adjudicating between different narrative accounts of origins, religions, etc., is simply not possible (Christian Smith 2003, see especially chapter 4).

On the other hand, it is entirely possible that Resisters do understand what Lyotard had in mind and since in the final analysis they believe that there *is* a universal reason that legitimates all knowledge, even their belief in, and knowledge of, God, that they accurately understand that a belief in universal reason is hard to sustain in light of empirical evidence and rival philosophical arguments, and so must argue that Lyotard is wrong in order to legitimate their own perspective. Whether the latter point is accurate or not, it is apparent through their remarkably similar definition of postmodernism across many different sources that in the service of getting their resistance message to resonate with the fears and concerns of the Christian world, they often play fast and loose with the perspectives with which they are in conflict, often taking terms, ideas, and concepts and setting them up for an easy critique. The result, however, is phenomenal, if by success we mean the degree to which the Resister understanding of postmodernism has been taken on by an ever larger segment of Christianity.

In the end, the relative success or failure of the Resisters remains to be seen. Although it might appear that their rationalistic perspective is doomed in the face of present-day challenges to such a worldview, they have proven adept at adapting their message and approach to changing cultural realities, through their use of language, an appeal to expert systems and encouraging intellectual endeavor among their followers (everyone wants to be thought of as smart, after all!), and through their embrace of both traditional technologies, such as radio and tapes (now CDs), and a variety of digital technologies, such as websites, online educational outlets, blogs, and podcasts, to name a few, to show that their message is rational, true, and even relevant to the new digital, dare we say, postmodern culture.

CHAPTER 5

Reclaimers

Protestantism is like a pup-tent outside
the Kingdom.

— Vanessa, adult convert to Catholicism

LOS ANGELES, CALIFORNIA

We arrived at the Orthodox church[1] at about
nine forty-five in the morning for the ten o'clock service.
Although we were only a few minutes early, hardly anyone was
outside on the church grounds, and only a few cars were in the
parking lot. Our plan was to attend the morning worship service, and then to meet up with several young adult converts to
Orthodoxy whom we had previously contacted, most of whom
attended this church. As we passed through the iron gate and
into the walled and cloistered courtyard, we were warmly
greeted by Harold, an elderly gentleman who had taken it upon
himself to make us feel welcome. Whether these were his official duties or not was unclear, but regardless, he was the only
one around, and he enthusiastically created a warm and inviting
first impression.

The church itself was a bit of a surprise. Sandwiched
between the foothills of Los Angeles and a major LA freeway,
adjacent to a community college and a large memorial park
that overlooks the church from the hills, the church building
was not what we had expected. In our minds we saw stained
glass, stone walls, domes topped with Orthodox crosses,
and arched doorways. What we saw was a small, stucco,

mission-style chapel, typical of many small neighborhood churches in southern California, with what appeared to be a small traditional Protestant cross over the small square tower topping the building.

As Harold showed us to our seats and pointed out the prepared guide to the Orthodox worship service that was kept in the pew shelf with the hymnals, we saw that the southwestern mission-style architecture continued into the interior of the building. There were dark wooden doors and window casings, wrought-iron chandeliers, and a small balcony in the rear of the room, with the added element of iconographic reliefs depicting various scenes from the life of Christ and the gospels mounted on the walls around the pews. Sunlight was streaming in through the windows, which were situated a good ten feet above the ground and ran the length of the sanctuary. This was another surprise. Perhaps we were expecting a dark and brooding atmosphere; instead, it was bright and light. In the front of the sanctuary, separating the nave from the rest of the space, was a newly completed chancel arch mural with three separate arches adjacent to each other and depicting, as described in the church literature, "Jesus Christ as Savior and Judge accompanied by the angels of the last judgment," Michael and Gabriel, flanking Jesus on either side. Over each arch were the words "Christ is Risen," in English over the center arch and in Greek, Latin, Arabic, and Russian over the two other arches. The colors were rich hues of blue, red, and gold, the artistry by a renowned Orthodox iconographer—finally something that looked like what we expected an Orthodox church to look like!

As the ten o'clock hour approached, the small sanctuary gradually began to fill with a diverse congregation, parishioners young and old, male and female, and representing many different ethnicities. We soon began to smell the incense and could see the smoke illuminated in the bright sunlight streaming through the windows. We turned to see the priest and his attendants preparing to enter the sanctuary, and just as they began their processional march, with both the smoke and the fragrance of the incense becoming more and more intense, we realized that the hymn to which they would enter was the nineteenth-century Protestant hymn "Beneath the Cross of Jesus." With the organ playing the strains of the song and the congregation beginning to sing, we looked at each other and silently agreed that this was definitely not the type of music we were expecting, but as we looked back to the front of the sanctuary, our eyes fell upon the large crucifix hanging over the altar in plain view of everyone in the room, giving a new urgency to the words of the song. Other similar Protestant hymns were used throughout the service. "When Morning Guilds the Sky" and "Fairest Lord Jesus," among others, brought more to mind the heyday of American Protestantism in the last century, especially revivalists like Billy Graham and others, than an Orthodox liturgy.

The service itself was not unlike a Catholic or Episcopal worship service. Because we recognized the hymns, it reminded us of other services we had attended, albeit with the necessities and symbols of the Orthodox faith, which in themselves were sufficient to make the worship service a bit confusing and required quite an effort for the uninitiated to follow along. The different rhythm and cadence of the service, wondering what exactly were all those priests doing in that sacred and set apart place behind that new archway, and just trying to figure out what might come next made us relieved as the service came to a close. On this note, it is interesting that several Orthodox churches we have investigated include on their websites an article by Frederica Mathewes-Green, herself a convert to Orthodoxy, titled "First Visit to an Orthodox Church—Twelve Things I Wish I'd Known." Talking later, our wish was that we had known of that article before we made our initial visits, although experiencing the services "cold" and reading later the explanation of what went on did provide its own unique perspective on the experience.

After the service, we were invited to enjoy a parish luncheon with the congregation, provided by the church and served
by the women of the parish. Virtually everyone stayed after the
service for the luncheon, which had an informal community,
even family, feeling and included several announcements of
birthdays and other items of interest to the congregation. As we
ate lunch, several parishioners approached the Father, and their
respect and reverence for him was apparent, as was his care and
concern for each of them. During this time we were able to
meet and talk informally with several parishioners, all of whom
showed interest in us and in our project, and we were made to
feel welcome in their community.

Following lunch, we gathered together the individuals we
had previously contacted and walked back over to the sanctuary
for a quiet place in which to give them more information about
our project, and to see if they might be interested in spending
some time telling us about their journey to the Orthodox faith.
The conversation started off well. We gave a basic overview of
our project, and each of the young parishioners introduced
themselves, gave a brief description of their conversion to
Orthodoxy (all of them had come from Protestant backgrounds), and expressed interest in engaging in a longer, more
detailed interview about their spiritual journey. After about an
hour of this conversation, the Father came into our meeting and
proceeded to ask several questions and comment on our project
and intentions, and in general attempted to play out his congregational patriarchal role with us, despite our role as researchers
who were not affiliated in any way with his church. For
example, after asking us what might be in it for the church to
participate in our study, he told us that he didn't think that it was
really our research project that had brought us to his church, but
the Holy Spirit, and implied that our spiritual lives were in need

of being fulfilled—indeed could only be fulfilled—in the Orthodox Church, presumably his church in particular.

The Father's approach to us, our project, and our "real" reason for being at his church, as well as his line of questioning, changed the previously open atmosphere and the willingness of the young converts to tell us their stories. We soon realized that because of the Father's approach we would most likely not be able to interview any of these young people, but also that the interaction would be interesting and instructive, however it ended up. One young man who had recently completed his master's degree in the philosophy of religion, and who had already agreed to tell us the story of his spiritual journey, was apparently emboldened by the Father's questioning of us. Following the Father's lead, he proceeded to tell us that in fact our questions about their journey to the Orthodox faith were the wrong questions, and that it would be pointless to have a conversation about his or any of their journeys to Orthodoxy, since the answer to our question was that it was the Holy Spirit who had brought them to the Orthodox Church, the one true church in his view, and sociological and psychological variables were irrelevant to that process. As one of our research assistants observed later, if that were true, why then weren't all Christians Orthodox? Wouldn't the Holy Spirit then bring all people of good faith to the Orthodox Church if it is the only true expression of Christianity? In the end, the Father refused to give permission to his parishioners to tell their stories to us, forbade us to talk to them, and we had no further contact with the Father or any of the young people at his church.

We include the details of this story, including the refusal of the Father to grant permission to his charges to speak with us, not to disrespect either the Father or his church, but rather because the experience illustrates, albeit in a somewhat exaggerated sense, several characteristics of what we found among those

we have interviewed and have grouped into the type we are calling "Reclaimers." We detail these patterns below, but briefly
they include: a desire for order and structure, indeed limits to
belief and actions, including a spiritual mentor—Father
even—who will set these limits; a sense of participating in a
larger piece of Christian history and tradition than what they
had previously experienced, often with the result of framing
their current tradition as the best, or most true, or most historically vital, expression of Christianity; and ultimately, among
many of those we are calling Reclaimers, a sense of a superior
spirituality to all others (that is, the idea often expressed is anal-
ogous to the Father's suggesting that our visit to his church was
the result of the Holy Spirit bringing us there for our spiritual
good, that once one becomes a convert to Orthodoxy, or
Episcopalianism, etc., one is then enlightened to the limitations
and foibles of all other expressions of Christianity). As the epigraph at the opening of this chapter suggests, from the perspective of many Reclaimers, other forms of Christianity are seen as
significantly less developed than are these liturgical forms of
Christian expression.

CONTEXT

Much has been written recently about a return to "orthodox" religious traditions, both among young adult Christians
(Carroll 2002) and more generally within and across the different Christian traditions and within Orthodox Judaism (Oden
2003). Colleen Carroll has written of "the new faithful," young
adults who have come to embrace an orthodox expression of
Christianity, whether through an intentional spiritual search or
through a "critical reflection on their current beliefs and practices" (2002, 17). Among the characteristics of the young
believers Carroll identifies are a personal identity that is centered
in their religious beliefs, a worldview that challenges core values

of the dominant secular culture, an adherence to traditional morality and religious devotion, a yearning for mystery, and a seeking for guidance from "legitimate" sources of authority (2002, 15–16). Carroll argues that what sets these young people apart from other believers is their conscious, intentional commitment to their beliefs, despite "external obstacles or internal doubts" (2002, 18). Similarly, Drew University theologian Thomas Oden has written about what he sees as a broader embrace of orthodox teachings by "seekers" within both Christianity and Judaism, who in their seeking have "a passion for roots, a yearning for depth, an appetite for prudence, a longing for tradition," resulting in a "profound rediscovery of the texts, methods, and pastoral wisdom of the long-neglected rabbinic and patristic traditions" (2003, 10–11).

But there is a somewhat longer history of reclaiming ancient orthodoxies than either Carroll or Oden imply, primarily as found in several sources that recount the personal faith journeys of individuals who have discovered different liturgical traditions and subsequently converted to Episcopalianism, Eastern Orthodoxy, or Catholicism. For example, Robert Webber, writing in the mid-1980s, documented what he saw as a move from evangelicalism to the Episcopal church (1985). In this, he documented his own spiritual journey, and included the stories of several others who had followed a similar path. Based on his own and these other stories, Webber identifies six reasons why evangelicals are attracted to the Episcopal church. First, there is a desire for a return to mystery, in contrast to the "rationalistic Christianity" of evangelicalism; second, a desire for an experience of worship in which the believer actively participates in worship as an experience of God; third, a desire for "sacramental reality," or experiencing the mystery of God through the sacraments of the church; fourth, the search for a Christian identity that extends beyond the history of evangelicalism or even Protestantism; fifth, an ecumenism that celebrates the "unity in diversity" of the different perspectives within the Episcopal church; and sixth, the development of a spirituality that embraces belief, ethics, and experience rather than simply beliefs and right behavior.

From within the Orthodox tradition, there have been several published accounts of conversions to Orthodoxy, both individuals and entire congregations. Peter Gillquist (1992) details the journey taken by former Campus Crusade for Christ staff members, away from evangelicalism, that resulted in the conversion of two thousand former Protestants to Orthodoxy. Their journey was undertaken as an intentional quest for the "New Testament Church," which in their view was not represented in any form of Protestantism or Catholicism. This journey, beginning in the late 1960s, took several years and ultimately resulted in their establishing the Evangelical Orthodox Church, which included several congregations across the United States, and which in 1987 was accepted into the Antiochian Orthodox Christian Diocese of North America (Lucas 2003, 7).

Gillquist also published an edited volume of the conversion narratives of several former Protestant clergy, documenting their conversions to the Orthodox Church (1992). When reading the conversion accounts of these ministers, several of the same themes that Robert Webber identified as attractions for evangelicals to the Episcopal church are readily apparent. For example, Thomas Renfree, who made his way to Orthdoxy from the Methodist church of his youth, through evangelicalism and Campus Crusade for Christ, and who is now an Orthodox priest, notes the lack of any "sacramental theology" within evangelicalism, which thus "accept[s] by default a form of worship based on the entertainment and/or lecture models of our modern age rather than upon any kind of biblical model" (1992, 57). Timothy Cremeens, an Orthodox priest in Brooklyn, and a convert from Pentecostalism, points up the difference between a Pentecostal worship service that emphasizes one's personal

experience of the Holy Spirit and the experiential but historically situated worship of the Orthodox Church:

> Some elements of Pentecostal/charismatic worship are
> based on the emotions. If the worship service turned out to
> be a "good one," the Holy Spirit must have been present.
> However if one didn't 'feel' right about worship, then
> perhaps the Holy Spirit was absent. Much of Pentecostal/
> charismatic worship and spirituality is grounded in this
> highly-subjective experiential mode. . . . However, while
> worship in the Orthodox Church is certainly experiential,
> incorporating all of our human senses, it is not based upon
> one's emotions, creative spontaneity, or the personality
> of the worship leader. Instead it is based upon the time-
> honored and time-tested words and actions of the Apostolic
> Church. (1992, 92–93)

Finally, Ron Olson, a former evangelical missionary to
Colombia who currently runs an Orthodox inner city mission
in a predominately Hispanic neighborhood, where he and his
family also live, notes that within Orthodoxy mystery and the
unknown are not only accepted, but even encouraged through
Orthodox theological teachings. He says that in contrast to
"rationalistic Western theology, Orthodoxy leaves room for the
unknown and teaches it is okay to look upon God as a mystery."
He continues that from the Orthodox perspective, God cannot
"merely be systematized, analyzed, and synthesized at will"
(1992, 139).

Two other Orthodox conversion accounts should be noted
here, as each of these individuals has long had a presence across
broad segments of American Christianity. Frank Schaeffer, formerly known as Franky, the son of mid-twentieth-century evangelical guru Francis Schaeffer, and who had made a bit of a
splash for himself within conservative Christian circles in the

early 1980s with his books aimed simultaneously at criticizing
the Christian church and the secularity of American culture
(see, e.g., Schaeffer 1981; 1982; 1984), details his spiritual journey, similar to those above, ultimately finding the historic
Christianity of the Orthodox Church (2002). Schaeffer maintains the combative tone he developed in his "culture wars" days
of the 1980s, and takes an even more pronounced stance than
either Gillquist or the contributors to his edited volume in his
claims that the one true church can only be found within
Orthodoxy.

Not only does Schaeffer argue for the superiority of
Orthodoxy over Protestantism and Catholicism, he also criti-
cizes the ethnic/immigrant Orthodox Church of being "ethnic
clubs," being spiritual "dead wood," and ultimately for not
being true to their commitment to the Orthodox faith. He
argues that the Orthodox Church needs to be revitalized, presumably through converts like himself, and in order to do so
"the Church must be given new life, not by political means, but
by prayer and passionate spirituality within the Church as practiced by those who *do* care about their faith, their children, their
Church and the defense of our unique sacramental tradition."
He concludes by calling the "Orthodox faithful" to a "quiet
revolution . . . of the spirit against the horror of today's relativism which renders all things unstable, inhuman and unwork-
able. It is a revolution in which, step by step, convert by convert,
the failures of the corrupted Roman Catholic Church and the
reactionary 'Reformation' it inevitably spawned are *lovingly but
firmly* corrected" (2002, 310–11 [emphasis in original]).

Frederica Mathewes-Green (1997), a popular Christian
writer and convert to Orthodoxy who has written in a wide
range of media, from books to regular columns in such media
outlets as Beliefnet.com and *Christianity Today*, and also has been
a commentator on NPR, uses the Orthodox calendar as a framing device to talk about her (and her family's) journey to the

Orthodox Church, and to implicitly invite others to become curious about the mysteries inherent in Orthodoxy and to seek them out for themselves. Her book is a witty and obviously loving account of her experience in the Orthodox Church that is focused simultaneously on its rituals and symbolism and her own sometimes bumpy journey into Orthodoxy. Where Gillquist and Schaeffer present a more forceful argument for Orthodoxy as the one true church, Mathewes- Green invites the reader to vicariously experience it through her account, and ultimately she hopes readers will find their own way into a church that is "challenging, strong, and true," thus offering a more subtle appeal for Protestant Christians (and others) to come into the Orthodox Church (1997, xx; on developing ancient spirituality, see also Mathewes-Green 2001).

What these conversion accounts share with the studies from Carroll and Oden, and with our findings, is that all of them express a desire to have an embodied religious experience, a more direct involvement in the worship and life of the parish, and a sense of participation in a larger history of Christianity, usually without giving up a conservative theological and social-moral belief system (see O'Neill 1987 for similar Catholic conversion accounts; see also Cimino 1997 for similar themes across these traditions). In a sense, there is a desire among converts to have certain "add-ons," the "smells and the bells" that are not available in the traditions from which they came, without having to change their general worldview. Certainly there is a bit of a learning curve for these converts as they first seek to understand just what is going on in a Catholic, Episcopal, or Orthodox worship service, and more, what it actually means to *be* Catholic, Episcopal, or Orthodox, but these accounts suggest that this is something that the converts throw themselves into, and which drives their quest in many ways—to understand what in their view is a more authentic, historical expression of Christianity.[2]

Reading these conversion accounts for the enthusiasm the new converts show for their newfound faith, and for their implicit and explicit evangelistic tendencies, particularly in pointing out the shortcomings of different Protestant traditions for an authentic, historically true Christian life, they show how in many ways the groundwork was laid for what we are now observing to be a growing segment within Christianity. Combining the patterns we can discern from these conversion accounts with what others have found, and with our observations from our interviews with Reclaimers, this seems to be the result of three interrelated processes: First, after conversion, there is a definite evangelization impulse for these converts. This is a more explicit effort for the Orthodox converts, but even where this is not as obvious an effort or emphasis, there is generally an accompanying attitude that their newly found tradition is the right, best, true, etc., Christian expression that at least implies, and in many cases simply states, the historical and theological shortcomings of Protestantism. Second, the early converts established networks and institutions that are friendly to Protestant or other converts to their tradition, thus making it much easier to think about attending an Orthodox, Episcopal, or Catholic church when one realizes that the trail has been blazed by others, and that these others are easily found in congregations that are empathetic and understanding of the (potential) convert's journey. Third, these networks have been developed and expanded, and now function to draw people into the orbit of those who are involved in liturgical churches. For example, everyone we met and interviewed had been invited by a friend or acquaintance to visit a liturgical church or had been introduced to different literature from the liturgical traditions. At minimum, converts had been informally influenced by others, whether through friendships, work relationships, or mentor relationships, to consider one or another liturgical tradition (see Carroll 2002, 19, for her similar description of this process).[3]

It is also apparent that there is an educational effect at work here. All of the Reclaimers we interviewed, as well as those who have published accounts of their journey to the liturgical traditions, are college educated (or currently pursuing their college studies) and in many cases graduate school educated, at least through the master's degree level. Further, they all, in one way or another, expressed their desire to bring together the intellectual and spiritual aspects of their lives into a coherent whole, which from their perspective was not possible within the Protestant tradition. As a point of comparison, this is a similar desire, although with a quite different outcome, to that which the Resisters express, of trying to bring into coherence their intellectual and spiritual lives. Of course, Resisters end up with a completely disembodied and intellectualized, "rational" legitimation of Christianity and their spiritual lives, completely disregarding what we see Reclaimers (and in fact Innovators, and to some extent Appropriators as well) pursuing, a spirituality that involves the whole person—body, emotions, and the mind.

This desire to unite the mind and the heart, as it were, can also be seen in the rediscovery of ancient Christian teachings that is currently enjoying widespread appeal, and which we find across each of our types—again, excepting the Resisters, who focus on more modern, rationalist approaches to spiritual life. In this, the teachings of the Church Fathers, recent writings on the spiritual disciplines (see, e.g., Foster 1998; Willard 1988), and the popularity of spiritual retreats and spiritual formation programs can be found in a wide variety of Protestant congregations, and even in evangelical seminaries, that utilize these same methods and resources.[4] Again, we find these pursuits across the boundaries of our typology, especially here with the Reclaimers and also among the Innovators who are including in their spiritual quest a variety of resources from Ancient Christianity. However, it is only among the Reclaimers that we find a wholehearted embrace and a seeking out of the ancient traditions within the context of a particular Christian community that traces its roots to earlier forms of Christianity.

PATTERNS

We have called this type "Reclaimers" because it includes individuals who are all, in one way or another, seeking to renew their experiences of Christianity through the history, symbolism, and practices of ancient traditions of Christianity, such as are still found in the liturgical traditions, particularly the Episcopal, Orthodox, and Catholic churches, thus *reclaiming* the ancient symbols, rituals, and practices of these traditions for their own spiritual quest. These are converts, either from other, nonliturgical forms of Christianity or from nonexistent or lapsed faith commitments. In this, the particular attractiveness of these traditions are the symbols, rituals, and smells of these churches, as well as the small congregational communities of believers that they represent, the connection to a larger historical tradition within Christianity, and the perceived authenticity that these traditions provide.

In our interviews and visits to our respondents' churches, we found five primary characteristics of those who are seeking to reclaim the rituals and traditions of the liturgical churches. First, there is an attraction to the visual and ritualistic elements of liturgical churches, including the physical embodiment that these require; second, they articulate a desire for a connection to a larger history of Christianity than what they had previously known in their spiritual lives; third, there is an attraction to and desire for a small religious community; fourth, they exhibit a desire for and commitment to a strict spiritual regimen, including confession and cultivating spiritual disciplines; and finally, we find a desire for "religious absolutes" and a set social structure which these Post-Boomers find within these congregations.

Attraction to Visual and Ritual

The attraction to the visual and ritualistic elements of the liturgical churches is at least partly self- evident in that these traditions have historically provided a visual link to Christian teachings—what one Episcopal priest we interviewed called "audio-visual aids to understanding the gospel," which ranges from stained glass, icons, and incense, to kneeling, genuflecting, and the kissing of icons and touching of priests' garments. All of these elements were identified as being partially responsible for attracting these people to these traditions—the visually compelling, embodied experience of the sacred that is available to them every time they attend a service at their church.

At the Episcopal Church of the Blessed Sacrament in suburban Orange County, California, the rector, Father David Baumann, was curious as to why over two dozen college

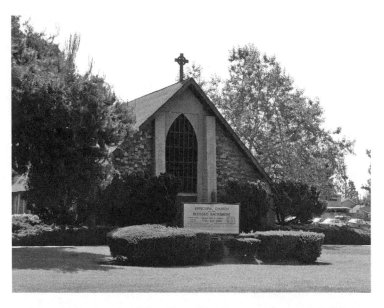

5-1. Episcopal Church of the Blessed Sacrament, Placentia, California. Photo by Richard Flory.

students from a nearby evangelical Christian college had over the past few years descended upon his church, making it their spiritual home. He identified Blessed Sacrament as an "Anglo-Catholic, high-Mass-on-Sunday church," and seemed genuinely amazed that young people from Baptist, Assemblies of God, Christian and Missionary Alliance, and similar backgrounds, none with any experience in liturgical churches, would throw themselves so completely into parish life, transforming themselves, and the church, in the process.

According to Father Baumann, when he asked the students what had attracted them to the church and why they remained, the students responded in remarkably similar ways. Many of them first described their dissatisfaction with their experiences in evangelical churches, and then in various ways expressed their attraction to the ritual, experiential, and visual elements that make up the mass at Blessed Sacrament, as well as the importance of the connection to a larger Christian history than what is usually emphasized in evangelical churches.

For example, Emily, a sophomore at the college, stated that she had considered attending an Episcopal church because she was dissatisfied with the "God is my teddy bear/best friend mentality of many evangelical churches." Rebecca, also a sophomore, gave a similar response: "I began looking into more liturgical styles of worship [because] I was fed up with the seeker-friendly Willow Creek movement, and remembering a missions trip to Russia, I looked into the Orthodox Church and other liturgical styles." This is not to suggest that these two young women really understood beforehand what an Episcopal mass was going to be like. One of the students, Emily, for instance, noted that she was at first a bit confused with all the liturgical activity taking place, but despite her initial confusion she was "wholly conscious of God's presence," and over time she began to "understand through experience what sacraments were and what it meant to experience grace so tangibly." She concluded that she is "learning to experience God with my heart as well as my head."

Overwhelmingly, these students—all between the ages of eighteen and twenty-three—expressed that what they found at Blessed Sacrament was a Christian tradition that, through its liturgy, demonstrated a connection to a much larger history than was held by their evangelical churches, and that the liturgy itself allowed them to experience God in ways they had never imagined. Some, like David, a senior at the college, simply made the case that Blessed Sacrament "provides an atmosphere for me to worship God using my whole being—body, soul, and mind. The liturgical style helps me to focus on my soul and mind by also engaging my body. This allows me to focus on God and remember his holiness in a real and meaningful way." Others, like Charity, a first-year college student, expressed the same sentiments but with a more graphic sense of discovery. She said, "I love the incense. I've been wanting to burn some ever since I heard this song about 'the prayers of the saints being sweet smelling incense to God's heart.' I love the kneeling, the silence—especially at the beginning of the service when people can pray. I love the hymns and am learning to read music. I like having communion every week and having one cup and bread and going up to the front to get it. I like bowing and genuflecting." Still others were impressed by the visual nature of mass, the accouterments, and even the church grounds. Heather, a sophomore, said:

> The first thing that I noticed on my first Sunday was the incredible beauty. Everything, the liturgy, the vestments, the church itself, the grounds, was beautiful, and obviously intended to be that way. It was so wonderful to be in a church that saw beauty as something important, something to be enjoyed for its own sake because it is a reflection of God, rather than something that is tacked on as an

afterthought. And the beauty was not just observed, it was experienced. The incense, the spoken and sung liturgy, the kneeling, the Eucharist itself, all demanded participation in the beauty of the worship. It was like being in the orchestra instead of watching a performance.

Becca, who is twenty years old, related her attraction to the liturgy at Blessed Sacrament and compared it to her experiences in other nonliturgical Protestant churches:

> Finding reverence for God and order to the worship and something that didn't deny that you had a body was important. A lot of times I felt like I went to a sort of Gnostic or dualist church that was interested in your soul and that was it. It didn't care that you had a body, you know, it was nice that you had a body but your body is going to die and disintegrate and you're not going to see it again. I always had this feeling that that was somehow wrong, so when we would kneel and stand and genuflect and cross ourselves it was just like, "Wow, what I do with my body matters in the life of my soul and the life of my soul matters to my body." It was exciting to find a church that just understood this and then had the tradition.

Becca continued, discussing the tactile dimensions of the worship at Blessed Sacrament:

> So there's incense, which you smell and there's the wine and the bread, which you taste, and everything that you see. And then you hear the bells and you hear the songs and the organ, and you touch things. I mean it's a sensory overload at first when you're coming from a more evangelical church where you don't have all of that. So I think that your body has a lot to do with the worship and perhaps even with the people's joy that we see around us. So when you go to

Blessed Sacrament and you smell things and you hear things and touch things and you taste things, it's like, "Oh," suddenly you're in the part of the museum where you get to play with stuff.

Similar sentiments were expressed by members of St. Barnabas Orthodox Church, also in southern California. Debra and Derrick Sanser, both in their mid-thirties and with three children, are typical in both their spiritual searching and their understanding of the Orthodox Church. They had previously been members of several Protestant churches, such as the Vineyard and Calvary Chapel, yet always seemed to be searching for the permanence and richly textured experience they have finally found in the Orthodox Church. Debra said that on their first visit to St. Barnabas "the room was filled with incense and the choir just really inspired me. . . . When we walked in I was holding [our daughter] and we were standing in the back and she said, 'Mommy, God is here.'" Derrick, contrasting St. Barnabas to his experience in Protestant churches, said, "you see icons visually, you smell the incense, everything is sensory. . . . We're not sola scriptura [like the Protestants]. Jesus came in human form to restore human flesh, so being human is not a bad thing. Its actually being restored is a good thing, so we're actually holistic about that."

Connection to a Larger History of Christianity

Virtually everyone we interviewed, regardless the tradition they had discovered and converted to, expressed a consistent rhetoric that their tradition was the "One True Church" that can be traced to the apostolic era. This can manifest itself in a more- or less-strong form, usually with the Orthodox converts having the strongest responses, framing any Protestant churches as having little or no history or set structure, and the Orthodox being the most ancient, most authentic Christian tradition. Erin, a twenty-year-old who attends St. Barnabas and recently became more actively committed to church and the Christian faith, said,

> I've realized that we can actually trace our church back to Antioch, which is where they first called Christians, Christians. So, to me that's amazing. Not many people can do that with their faith, and it doesn't change. It's the same liturgically, you know, through the years. Like the chanting and the prayers, it's not made up. The prayers that we pray and all the chants have been written down through the years by saints or monks or, you know, the forefathers, all that. And, they spent their entire life, you know, trying to seek the true church and it just seems like, again, it's been passed down and it's something that's so real and very, very tangible. In the other church, it was just very, again, you say whatever came to your mind and it just seemed odd.

Benny Wisenan, a thirty-year-old schoolteacher whom we interviewed at St. Barnabas along with his sister, Ruth Rutledge (he is a member of another Orthodox Church in the area), framed this in the sense of finding a new source of roots in an otherwise mobile and history-less society, saying, "you know [in southern California], the oldest buildings are like the 1950s, so I never felt rooted, you know, and I became Orthodox here in touch with cultures that are thousands of years old, that have been Christian since, you know, if it's the Greeks or the Antiochians, they have been Christians since Pentecost. And the Russians have been Christians since the 600s and they have these deep traditions and now I'm a part of that. And it really gave me a sense of being part of something, whereas before I was kind of lost."

The Sansers framed it as providing a sense of continuity, in that wherever they may happen to be, the liturgy will be exactly the same: "in the beginning of our discovery of the Orthodox Church, we visited all the area Orthodox churches and they did the same things each night of the week in each church. . . . We even visited a Greek church in Chicago not long thereafter. They said the same liturgy completely in Greek, and we understood, we knew what was going on. No matter where you go, or what time or what year or what age, it's the same."

Providing a somewhat softened version of this, Lindsey, one of the college students at Blessed Sacrament, said that she enjoyed the liturgy because "it's ancient. I mean in its earliest forms it comes from the early church hiding out in the Roman Empire and the Apostles. . . . It's passed the test of time, and it's carried the doctrines through." Similarly, Becca said that "going to a church that's been doing the same thing for almost two thousand years or the Episcopal church for five hundred years is like, 'Somebody thought a long time about this, and we've gotten rid of stuff that doesn't work and we're sticking to stuff that does.' . . . It can feel a little repetitive sometimes . . . but if you really engage in worship you realize that you're being led by millions of people before you who have said these things and who have done these things, and you're not just wandering around in your twenty-something arrogance trying to plow your own path." Amy, also at Blessed Sacrament, suggested that although the liturgy might seem to be the product of rote repetition when first encountered, she found that it has great value in her spiritual life. She said she initially had "this reaction that it's so rigid, it's so formal, they do the same thing every week . . . but one of the things that I found as I continued coming here was that the form of the worship was the same and that didn't change, and it was always steady and sort of comforting, it allowed me the freedom to worship better than I have ever been able to before because it wasn't all about me, it was about everybody in the church worshipping together communally."

Mark, a thirty-one-year-old teacher and convert to the Episcopal church, framed it this way: "I said, 'Now, wait a second. These are the churches that have the history; these are the churches that go back to the first centuries. If they're all the same like this, this is surely of apostolic origin. This cannot be of anything else.' I'm now in a church that is in direct apostolic succession, and this sense of joining this enormous body of believers that transcends time and space is very powerful. I'm not a part of something that's just for today, just for my generation, I'm part of something much bigger."

Desire for Small Community

The desire for a small community within which they are known, are active, and to which they are responsible is a consistent desire for these young people. In some cases this almost becomes a total world, in that they seem to be spending the majority of their time in or at the church. But in general, the desire to be known and to know other parishioners in an intimate way, and to be a part of a spiritual family, is the primary theme expressed. As one young woman at Blessed Sacrament told us, "It's really good to be in a place where I say the same words as people older than me, as people younger than me, that brings us together as a community, as a family, on the same level."

At St. Barnabas, Debra Sanser gave a similar expression of the role of the congregation in her life, seeing the church as an extension of the family:

> As a church we're meant to be the body of Christ, not just a bunch of individuals with our own private relationship. Of course we need to have a personal relationship with God. God has to be personally real for us. I think he intends that, but it's not only that. He gives us a bit of himself and expects us to share it with each other and to be a community together. I'm very happy when I come on Sunday morning and I see my godchildren and it gives me joy. And I feel like the church as a community looks out for each other's kids and everybody really looks out for each other.

If somebody's having a problem, people are there to help
you. . . . I think that's so essential in life.

Meanwhile, Benny Wisenan sees it in more spiritual terms: "in
the Orthodox Church I have this sense that the whole community is helping me with my salvation. They pray for me. The
saints intercede for me. We come to the liturgy all together in
communion and it's not, you know, it's not about works but
we're all interceding for each other. And so I feel like I'm not
alone." Similarly, Micah Snell, who along with his wife,
Jennifer, was one of the first of the students to begin worshipping at Blessed Sacrament and is now attending an Episcopal
seminary, said that when they first started attending Blessed
Sacrament, "We had an agreement that what we wanted to
find . . . was a church that we felt we could be a part of. . . .
One of the things we were really seeking was not to be a part of
a really big church that could fund any mission or program that
they wanted to put on—there is value in that—but what we
were looking for is the sense of family and a sense of belonging."
Jennifer added that she really valued the "family environment,"
where in her experience "people are not just putting on a smiling face and coming to church and saying how great their week
was, but where if there are hard things that happened, people are
honest, and that's been amazing to see the honesty and be able
to know that when people say they're going to pray for you, you
know they will."

High Commitment Level

The level of commitment needed to maintain the desired
spiritual regimen required, or at least expected, by these churches
is quite high. It is a bit misleading to say that there is a spiritual
regimen required by these churches, however. In fact, it is the
young people themselves who are seeking this sort of regimen
out, which is then provided by the priests and in the structure of

the available resources of the church traditions themselves. For example, among the converts to Orthodoxy that we have interviewed, the congregation in many ways has become the primary focus of their lives. For example, they often attended services three to four times per week (a number which is even greater during, for example, the Christmas season or Pascha—Orthodox Easter), which in turn has increased their involvement in and commitment to the life of the congregation. They have also sought out their priests as spiritual mentors, who then impose certain regimens, such as prayer, reading the Bible or the Church Fathers, or something similar, and confession of their sins to the priest. Further, at least for the Orthodox converts, the worship services themselves require significant stamina in order to make it through what are generally two- to three-hour standing services, where most of those in attendance remain standing for the entire time. One parishioner told us that he views that physical sacrifice as a spiritual discipline, to stand and participate throughout the entire service.

Erin, at St. Barnabas, acknowledged that it is often difficult to maintain the level of spiritual discipline she desires. But she said that although it is difficult "to stay focused sometimes and to go to the services and to be fasting and to try and be steadfast. I think that I would not be as into the faith if I hadn't been Protestant before because I was able to compare and contrast the two. I had to say, 'I don't feel comfortable with the Vineyard, but I do believe in God. This is what I do believe. This is what I want.'" Benny Wisenan, while similarly acknowledging the difficulty of maintaining a rigorous spiritual life, found help in his relationship with his priest:

> You have a relationship and you know you're accountable because if you're going to take it seriously you know that whatever you do you're going to have to reveal it to this person. Like the rule of prayer. There's the fasting

guidelines. There's church services. We have church on Saturday night, Sunday mornings. There's also various festival days we'll have during the week sometimes. There are other canons about various aspects of your life, and they all kind of sync with obviously the Gospels and the commandments and Christ's words and his teachings. If I have no structure and if I had no goals I could be very happy with myself and be content just to be as I am, but here I have this goal of this other thing of evening prayers and doing that consistently or morning and evening prayers; even a little bit doing that consistently is a tough thing to do to break habits and to build new habits . . . and you fail at that and then you go back, you know, to church, to Father, and you're admitting to this, "I can't even do three minutes a day or one minute a day; I'm not even faithful on that."

At Blessed Sacrament, Father Baumann said that among the many young people who have been attending over the past few years, several are on a similar path of pursuing a rigorous spirituality. He said:

> One of the things that they sought a lot is personal counseling, mentoring, spiritual direction, a good number of them are making their confessions; they're bringing in the real depth of their spiritual struggles. They're kind of like going through stages. You know the first few months, they were saying, "This is really great. It's so exciting. I can't wait to get here because all this stuff is going on and I really feel a part of it." And then the next stage is kind of, "I understand part of this now and I'm really enjoying my part of the ministry and getting the teaching and I want to bring my friends in and I'm seeing this as a real depth of satisfaction." And the third stage is, "I really feel God moving in my life and I want to make some major changes and rededicate my life to Christ. I want to make my confession. I want to come to

you for spiritual direction. I want some guidance. I want a
deeper prayer life. These are the sins that have been part of
my life for a long time. What can I do to combat that."
They are really seriously seeking deep sanctification.

Set Structure and Religious Absolutes

The desire for a set social structure and religious "absolutes"
within the context of the visual and embodied spiritual elements
that these churches provide was also almost universal in our
interviews. In general, it seems that there is an elective affinity
between the conservative natures of either the liturgical tradition into which one converts—Orthodoxy—or the particular
congregation that one finds—Episcopal—and the religious perspective of the Post-Boomer converts. That is, both tradition/
congregation and individual tend to be conservative religiously,
essentially finding a more culturally acceptable context in which
to be "fundamentalists," of a sort, but without the label.

Father Baumann reported that the young converts in his
church were saying, "We want absolute truth. We want the basic
gospel. We don't want to be entertained, we want to be challenged.
We want to be called to sanctity. We want to be challenged to
the moral life. We want to learn how to pray." Nate, one of the
students at Blessed Sacrament, sees dangerous trends in some of
the emerging forms of evangelical worship (which are similar to
what we have found in our Innovators) that are sometimes
framed as "postmodern" worship and that are being pursued
among his friends:

I tried to explain to them why you need, you know, some
kind of structure because you need to go somewhere with
this thing. You cannot have four hours of worship without
a point. . . . You need to have something to grasp on; you
need a central concept. They're like, "Well, God is the central concept." And it seems like they've learned all different

kinds of worship . . . but it's a very nebulous form and there's nothing to grasp hold of. It's not like at Blessed Sacrament, where you really can't just sit there or you'd be, you know, definitely be the odd man out, [where] you aren't part of the family if you were not participating in this ritual.

His fellow student and Blessed Sacrament member Lindsey agreed, and sees the structure of the liturgy as a guard against such changes. She said, "it's scary that postmodernism has crept into the church. . . . You know, there are areas in our spiritual lives that we can't even tell that we're being postmodern about it or deviating at all and we are. And one thing I like about the structure of the liturgy and things like that is [that] it's ancient.

5-2. Father Josiah Trenham, St. Andrew Orthodox Church, Riverside, California. Photo by Richard Flory.

5-3, Christina D., a convert to Orthodoxy at a sanctuary dedication service, St. Andrew Orthodox Church, Riverside, California. Photo by Richard Flory.

It has passed the test of time and it's carried the doctrines through. . . . Just the words themselves are so rich . . . It makes it more [difficult] to deviate from it."

Father Josiah Trenham, the thirty-four-year-old priest of St. Andrew Orthodox Church in Riverside, California, described both his interpretation of the mainline Presbyterian denomination in which he was raised and the advantage that the Orthodox Church has in comparison, particularly in terms of an unchanging structure and moral expectations:

> There was no continuity. There's nothing holding this together. My conclusion was the Protestant traditions, and I examined every one, Lutherans have done the same thing, Presbyterianism, Evangelicalism is way past, I mean not even close with regard to maintaining a culture, but these mainline churches have all gone through radical, radical

change, redefining what they believe constantly, writing new confessions, and as a Presbyterian we were doing that. I mean really, we were, the church I grew up in was subscribing to a new standard that was in contradiction to the Westminster Confession of Faith. How could you do that? Does Christianity change? Does doctrine change? And if doctrine changes, I mean, how do you know anything you believe is true? So the whole question of authority was kind of at the bottom also. It was that that drove me, and as I began to read these books . . . one thing that [became] very clear is that the Orthodox faith has produced a culture that's substantial. It's not perfect by any means . . . but what we haven't done is altered our doctrine. . . . They're not up for grabs.

For Father Josiah, this also translates into specific requirements for how one is to present oneself in public and in church, especially for women: "We have a modesty dress code. Uh, as a matter of fact I'm something of a hard head on it. I mean I don't let any women come to the church to pray without sleeves. . . . So [if a woman comes to church with bare arms] I have my ushers . . . offer her a shawl to put over her shoulders. So, modesty, décor, reverence, these things exist, and St. Paul says, 'Our worship to God ought to be with reverence and awe.' This is how we ought to worship, and that wasn't my experience." Thus for Reclaimers, the structure that their specific tradition offers, particularly in terms of what they frame as an unchanging tradition and theology, and even the proper roles for priests and parishioners, provides a core of stability in a rapidly changing world.

SUMMARY AND CONCLUSIONS

Reclaimers evidence a quest that takes them on a journey to ancient Christian traditions in small, family oriented congregations through which they pursue their desire for spiritual development.

Through the different faith narratives and across the patterns we've discerned from Reclaimers, three points seem most important in summing up their journey. First, they are drawn to the visual and ritualistic, in particular how this allows a physical embodiment of their beliefs and commitments. For Reclaimers, their faith is made more alive when they are visually and bodily involved in the different elements of their chosen tradition. Touching the garments of the priest, physically kneeling, having the elements of the Eucharist mediated by the priest, experiencing the smoky aura and smell of the incense and the accompanying bells, all of these serve to make the Reclaimers aware of both their minds and their bodies as they worship God. Second, and related to the appeal of the visual and physical elements, they desire to be a part of a longer history and tradition of Christianity. They are in effect placing themselves in what they see as a long line of fellow Christians, who stretch back to the apostolic age. Thus the symbols and rituals have even more resonance for Reclaimers, as they are interacting with the same symbols and performing the same rituals as Christians have done for hundreds, even thousands of years. Finally, this long history of tradition and the attendant structure of the tradition, as well as its resources for spiritual development, continue to allow these Christian believers to pursue their spiritual journey.

It is important to note here that we find this approach to be similar in many ways to the response of those who are working hard to resist the influences of postmodern culture (see chapter four). There is a certain amount of "border crossing" that takes place between these two types (although with important differences), particularly through blogs, websites, publications, and various networks that have been developed. As with the Resisters, there is a fundamental moral conservatism among Reclaimers, particularly on such issues as abortion, euthanasia, sexuality, gender roles, and their insistence that their way is *the* correct expression of Christianity. Thus, for example, none of the individuals we interviewed would support abortion rights or right-to-die laws, and although most would not object to equal rights for homosexuals, at least in the abstract, none would be supportive of same-sex unions. Similarly, in terms of gender roles, while most of the women we interviewed either had or were planning a career, most would not be supportive of women in pastoral roles in their churches, and indeed there seems to be a desire for patriarchal authority that correlates with their desire for strong, set boundaries—between true and false, right and wrong, and men and women.

What is different between the Reclaimers and the Resisters is that, first, Reclaimers are dissatisfied with the nonliturgical forms of Protestantism with which they grew up, and have thus converted to other Christian traditions, whereas the Resisters are attempting to effect change within Protestantism. Thus where Reclaimers are leaving the Protestantism of their youth for what in their view are the richer and deeper traditions of the liturgical churches, Resisters are trying to reform Protestantism from the inside out through an emphasis on rational beliefs. Second, Reclaimers are not interested in a rationalized Christianity as are the Resisters; instead, they are particularly drawn to the mystery, embodiment, and physical and experiential dimensions of the liturgical traditions, and often cite the disembodied "rationalism" of most forms of Protestant beliefs as one reason why they have left the fold. The final difference is that although Resisters and Reclaimers would certainly be, on the whole, fellow travelers in terms of their diagnosis of the relativism and secularity of American culture, the Reclaimers are much less interested in establishing some sort of overarching "Christian worldview" or moral order on American society. Instead, their interest lies in effecting change, to the extent that they can, through their more purely religious pursuits, away from the political sphere.

From our perspective, it is still an open question as to whether these young converts will remain within these traditions, or further, whether this trend will continue. On the one hand, particularly among the younger of the converts we've interviewed and observed, it could be partly a function of their age and status in life. After all, we expect young people in college and for sometime thereafter to be seeking out what it is they actually believe, what their commitments are, and how they should go about pursuing these, often in a different way than their parents did when they were of a similar age. On the other hand, there are plenty of examples of full and long-term conversions where young people converted to one or another liturgical tradition sometime in their twenties, and have since then remained, with no desire to return to the church traditions in which they were raised.

It is important to note as well that there is created among Reclaimers an at least symbolically total world through a retreat into a mythical past of a pristine religious tradition. As Reclaimers expressed it to us, all of their community and spiritual needs are met in and through the various resources provided by the tradition and congregation, and as well, the congregation often functions as an extended family. They expressed a belief that all other religious and Christian traditions are inferior, theologically, historically, and morally, thus creating boundaries, both social-moral and religious, beyond which they do not venture. Further, in the interest of enlightening others, they consistently express these beliefs to others of different or no religious commitments. In a pluralistic and highly mobile and fluid society such as the United States, this seems a difficult world to maintain, but this in fact seems to be one reason why these traditions are attracting converts—for the experience of a close-knit and caring community of fellow believers that provides a spiritual and moral constant in a complex and changing world.

The ultimate result of this perspective is a form of fundamentalism that would never recognize itself as such. Martin Riesebrodt (1993) has argued that fundamentalism is a patriarchal protest movement that arises in the face of rapid social change, protesting what adherents see as threats to their religious and moral sensibilities. In a very real sense, this is what we have observed from our Reclaimers: a form of protest movement against a history-less and compromised Protestantism, and a last bastion of patriarchal certitude in an egalitarian and pluralistic world. As Father Josiah of St. Andrew Orthodox Church told us, "Orthodoxy stands as a hierarchical church in the midst of an egalitarian wasteland."

In the end, however, we believe that this is a significant development within Christianity, in that these young people are returning to ritual and tradition, especially in an otherwise "do-it-yourself" world of spirituality. Reclaimers find within these liturgical traditions, and in their particular congregations, the kind of spiritual home they need that also provides the close-knit family/community environment they seek. Christian community becomes a real experience not only on Sundays, but throughout the week as Reclaimers participate with each other in the life of their church.

CHAPTER 6

Conclusion

It's not about you.
—Rick Warren, *The Purpose-Driven Life*

IN THE EMERGING SOCIAL SCIENTIFIC LITERATURE on spirituality, analysts have largely framed "spirituality" as a counterpart to "religion," with the spiritual referring to the inner life, and the individualistic search for meaning, whether this is from within a particular religious tradition or traditions or from a religiously unaffiliated "spiritual but not religious" approach (e.g., Carroll and Roof 2002; Fuller 2001, Porterfield 2001; Roof 1993; 1999; Wuthnow 1998, 2001, 2003). Spirituality is thus alternately framed as a *search* for meaning, a *quest* for spiritual fulfillment and/or development, or a move from an understanding of the spiritual as a place of "dwelling" to one of "seeking," or even "shopping" (Roof 1993, 1999; Wuthnow 1998; 2001; 2003; Cimino and Lattin 1998). The individual and her or his spiritual journey is the referent rather than the religious congregation or community, and the metaphor is one of movement, development, or choice as opposed to stability or constancy in a particular tradition or community of faith.

This individualistic questing, searching, and seeking for spirituality and spiritual fulfillment does not necessarily connote a complete break with all commitments to religious communities of the past. Rather, although some remnant of the more stable past remains for the individual, these forms of spirituality are primarily to be understood as an individual search, or quest,

157

for spiritual growth, fulfillment, and understanding, with the religious community acting, to the extent that it has an active role, as a sort of inessential aid, or context, to this journey.

None of the four types we have presented in this book would fall neatly into any of these characterizations. For example, Innovators, while clearly seeking out ways to deepen and expand their spiritual lives, embark on a journey that is not simply individualistic. They embrace "postmodern" culture and seek out how best to be a Christian within that context, but their commitment is not just to their personal spiritual journey, it is also to the religious community through which their spiritual quest is to be pursued, and to the surrounding community as well. Similarly, Reclaimers are also seeking out a deeper, more personally meaningful spiritual life, primarily through a retreat into a protected and established religious structure and set of expectations; yet, like Innovators, they are committed to their community of faith and it is the community through which their quest is to be pursued. Appropriators, of each of these four types, seem to be the most similar to the individual questing suggested in the literature, and while their pursuits are certainly individualistic, there is also at least an acknowledgment of the need for aspects of the community, and that it has an important role in their spiritual lives, even if it is in the context of small affinity groups through which they share their experiences, needs, and desires. Resisters, in contrast to each of the other types, represent a sort of rearguard defensive action intended to rationalize and scientize Christian beliefs, with the goal of increasing their cultural status while simultaneously preventing young people and others from even embarking on a spiritual journey or quest because of their fear that such a journey might take them away from the sort of rational beliefs they see as crucial to Christianity.

Given that the description of an individualistic spiritual quest does not precisely fit the types we have been describing,

our goal in this concluding chapter is to develop an explanation
that will take into account the different approaches to religion
and spirituality that we have presented in this book. With that in
mind, there are several things we need to do in this chapter in
order to develop an alternate explanation. First, we will review
the major characteristics of each of the four types we have presented in order to point up similarities and differences between
them and show how each of these types, as different as they
are, are all responding to similar desires of young believers, in
particular the experience and embodiment of beliefs in worship,
service, and outreach. We will then provide snapshots of two
congregations that we believe are demonstrating how the different concerns and desires apparent in each of the different types
can be combined into one congregation as an approach to
Christian identity and mission. Finally, taking what we see as the
common emphases of each of the types we have been discussing,
we will argue that we are witnessing the emergence of a new
form of spirituality that recovers ritual, embraces the body and
experience, and seeks community for both belonging and as a
context for living out Christian beliefs.

Major Characteristics of the Types

Innovators show four basic patterns, first, that their worship
is primarily visual and experiential. This goes beyond just
contemporary music—although they do have that—to include
art-making, foot washing, or experiences such as an arts liturgy
or entering and exiting a tomb. Second, Innovators are interested in situating themselves as individuals and their churches/
ministries as serving their surrounding communities. Thus we
find Innovators, as one of the members of the Bridge Communities framed it, "taking the church to the community"
through, for example, various community arts programs, community assistance, and outreach programs. Third, Innovators are

far less interested in developing large-scale institutions, or even in developing institutions that need to be maintained over time. Their model is of an "organic" community that has a definite life cycle of birth, life, and perhaps, ultimately, death if the community ceases to be effective or authentic as they see it. Their interest is more locally and intimately focused, toward the community of believers and outward toward their host city. Fourth, Innovators work to create inventive uses of the history, traditions, and rituals of different Christian traditions, in some cases even going outside Christian traditions for a more physically and visually oriented practice. In this, we see Innovators encouraging the development of ancient spiritual disciplines, such as silence and contemplation, communion services reoriented around the relationships within the community, and even labyrinth walks as a community activity intended to promote the contemplation of God in their individual and collective lives.

Reclaimers show five basic patterns. First, they are drawn to the visual and the ritualistic elements of the liturgical traditions, such as the icons, the taking of the Eucharist, even the sameness of the order of the service in their own church each week, as well as in any other congregation in the same tradition in which they might worship. Second, the ritualistic elements of the liturgical traditions require them to engage not only intellectually with the symbolism inherent in the rituals, but also physically in performing the rituals, whether kneeling, genuflecting, kissing icons, or standing for two hours. Third, they articulate a desire to know and become a part of a larger/longer Christian history and its traditions. In this Reclaimers repeatedly emphasize that they are now part of a long line of believers who have gone before and who have participated in the same traditions and rituals in which they are now participating. Fourth, Reclaimers show a desire for developing a strict spiritual regimen that includes spiritual mentorship by the priest or some other person in their congregation and the confessing of sins to the priest, along with the attendant requirements following such a confession. There is in this a need to be accountable to another person, particularly someone who is viewed as living an authentic Christian life and who therefore has the authority to mentor and give direction to the young believer. Finally, and related to their desire for a strict spiritual regimen, Reclaimers demonstrate a desire for religious absolutes and set structures that dictate belief, roles, and behavior, including both theological teachings and traditional structures that give them a sense of social and cultural order in what is an otherwise disordered and egalitarian world.

Resisters show three essential patterns. First, they emphasize an understanding of Christianity that prioritizes the cognitive as the essential element of Christianity, reducing it almost completely to being composed of what one thinks and believes, and emphasizing the unique rationality of Christianity and Christian beliefs. In this, Christian believers are instructed that they need to be more "intellectual" in their approach to their beliefs, and that since God is a god of "reason and logic," he demands an intellectual, rational, and logical approach to him. Second, Resisters oppose postmodernism because from their perspective it is irrational and illogical, it promotes relativism in beliefs and behavior, lacks an established and appropriate authority structure and place for any form of belief such as practiced by Resisters, and worse, will, as one Resister put it, "seduce some of our most gifted young men and women" into ministries that emphasize style, icons, incense, and experience over rational, intellectual substance and "true spirituality." Third, Resisters are intent on "reestablishing" a "Christian worldview" as the reigning/dominant perspective for governing American culture and society. This at first glance appears to be like what has come to be understood as fundamentalism or evangelicalism; however, it is actually a very particular form of conservative American Christianity that owes less to the history of Protestant fundamentalism or evangelicalism in the United States (and is more similar to a disembodied and Protestanized Thomistic philosophy on the one hand, and Christian Recon-structionism or "Dominion Theology" on the other) than to the fundamentalism and evangelicalism of such figures as Billy Graham, or even J. Gresham Machen or Carl Henry, theologians they seek to claim in laying out their lineage.

Finally, Appropriators show two basic patterns, with several emphases that tend to adapt in response to changing cultural and religious environments. First, Appropriators, in the interest of getting ever more people in their pews, offer what is essentially the mall/consumption equivalent within their churches. They offer many points of entry, and there are many options for people who venture into one of these churches to select from, including not selecting any programming option, whether the person is already a Christian believer or a "seeker." Thus in an Appropriator setting, primarily because of their large stores of resources, we can see pretty much everything we've seen in each of the other types and more, with perhaps the exception of some of the more ritualistic elements of the liturgical traditions, although there are also appropriations of some aspects of the liturgical forms. Second, just as Appropriators have brought the mall/consumption ethic to their churches, so they have estab-lished presences in the malls and the entertainment marketplace with big events such as the Harvest Crusade and the Uprising events. In this Appropriators are offering what can be thought of as a T-shirt or consumption identity to both believers and potential believers through the different design stories embed-ded on the clothing, music, stickers, jewelry, and other acces-sories that can be purchased to model who they want to be. Appropriators are adopting larger cultural fashion and identity trends and reinterpreting them with a Christian identity and message. They also offer a sort of religious entertainment model, complete with the appropriate Christian identity markers like

T-shirts, hats, and various forms of popular music, that serves as a form of both "religio-tainment" and a sense of community, however thin and fleeting it may be. After all, when one is surrounded by forty thousand-plus fellow believers, even if they are cheering for the Christian motocross riders, it does provide a sense of identity with something bigger than just oneself.

Thus, Appropriators are savvy cultural observers, one might even say marketers, who are able to see what is appealing to current and potential Christian believers in both the larger culture and within the church, and then put their resources to work to appropriate these forms and develop them into the different types of program/ministry/worship/consumption offerings they provide. This results in a multitude of programs oriented toward attracting seemingly any segment of the public. In one sense, these churches are truly postmodern organizations. Their identity is based on appropriating the experiences, consumption patterns, and the need for belonging, as found in both the larger culture and in the Christian culture, and then marketing these back to their members, with the intent to provide a place for them to find individual fulfillment and shelter from life's difficulties.

RELATIONSHIPS BETWEEN THE TYPES

None of the four types that we have constructed and presented here should be understood as somehow having impermeable boundaries, with no one, or no institutions, found in one part of the typology and not found in any other. There are certainly many types of relationships, and "border crossers" within and between these different groups, and probably nobody—and no church or ministry—would be completely comfortable with being placed into any one of these types. However, the strength of any typology is that it allows an analysis that would otherwise not be possible by putting into comparison dominant characteristics that might not otherwise be as easy to discern. Further, and more practically, we believe that typologies such as we have developed here allow both organizations and individuals an opportunity to try to determine where they think they might be placed—that is, in terms of their own dominant characteristics—and thus perhaps engage in a bit of self-analysis. That said, there are at least three dimensions along which these four different types can and do relate to each other, and through which we can make comparisons: first, in their approach to the visual and experiential dimension of religion; second, in their understanding and emphasis on community; and third, in how they pursue their different outreach, missions, or social action programs.

First, on the visual and experiential dimension, both Innovators and Reclaimers emphasize their attraction to the visual and experiential elements of their particular church traditions. For Innovators, this is a much more fluid element that is often created, or reinvented, from week to week, while for the Reclaimers this is a part of the longer Christian tradition they seek. For each, the source of the appeal is the participation *with* the divine in the context of a particular faith community, as opposed to passively observing an experience produced by others. That is, they are not interested in a spectator type of spiritual experience where they come in, sit down, and watch the show; rather, they want to participate both physically and intellectually in the worship experience. For Appropriators, on the other hand, there is much more of the spectator approach to the visual and experiential. That is, it appears that Appropriators appreciate the visual, and can have a type of individualistic experience of the divine, however, the community and participatory experience of ritual is missing. Thus an Appropriator worship service might look much like an Innovator service, but in reality everything is done for them and it all leads to a sermon centered on and around the minister. The parishioners are not really participants in creating parts of that experience, other than as an internal, individual experience. For Resisters, the visual and experiential is one of the key elements of postmodern culture against which they position themselves. God, says philosopher J. P. Moreland—echoing Neil Postman— "is a God of the word," and thus can only be understood in relation to the written word; experience, emotion, visual symbols, rituals, and the like are not allowed for Resisters. What Resisters exclude from their approach is precisely what Innovators, Reclaimers, and to a degree Appropriators each intentionally emphasize, and what they repeatedly expressed to us, that "the word" was embodied in Jesus, and did not remain simply an abstract set of ideas.[1] Thus, Resisters are committed to an abstract rationalist belief system, while Innovators, Reclaimers, and Appropriators find such an approach unsatisfactory; instead they understand Christianity as entailing more than simply a commitment to "rationality" and a cognitive assent to "truth."

Community, for Innovators, is one of their most powerful motivators, both for participating in a particular congregation and then for working back out into the community through different ministries and programs that are created in the church. Innovators seek a small, like-minded community of believers with whom they can journey together in their spiritual lives, and through which to live out those commitments. One way to think about their communities is that they have relatively open boundaries. They welcome anyone who comes to their doors, and in fact seek out people in the community through their different programs, to both invite them in and meet them in the community. Appropriators have a similar emphasis on open boundaries, yet their efforts are largely intended to attract people to their church, and for them to find there what might be thought of as personal affinity support groups, as a way to improve their lives and to build a sense of community. For example, most large, seeker-type churches, and many smaller churches for that matter, have an emphasis on "small groups," which by and large are organized around similar interests of the participants in each group. Thus we find different programs and small groups to take the church member from cradle to grave, all operating in the same way of observing cultural trends and providing the appropriate community experiences for their members. For Reclaimers, community is found in the relatively closed boundaries not only of the particular congregation, but of the traditions, morals, and social roles that are a vital part of whichever liturgical tradition they have found. They invite others in, whether from other Christian traditions or not, but have, in many ways, retreated into small, totalistic communities in which they can find the sense of morality and community they miss in the larger world. Resisters have a similar emphasis on closed boundaries, which although drawn less formally in terms of historical traditions, are very real and powerful nonetheless. Indeed, we might think of the entire Resister enterprise as one of establishing and maintaining clear boundary markers that delineate who is and who is not an authentic, rational believer.

Finally, each of these types envisions its role in outreach/missions/social action in significantly different ways. For Innovators, a core part of their effort is to participate in, and with, their host communities and to be a welcoming and helpful presence in those communities. These efforts are primarily locally focused, although they don't necessarily exclude international efforts, and Innovators seem always to be creating new types of involvements, which the members themselves, rather than paid church staff, are busy organizing. For Reclaimers, their efforts in these areas seem to be primarily whatever missions or other programs that the particular congregation or denomination supports. In fact, we heard hardly any mention of missions, or outreach, or social action in our interviews with Reclaimers or in visits to their churches. Their emphasis was primarily internal to the congregation and the tradition. For Resisters, missions efforts involve almost exclusively an emphasis on changing ideas, both the ideas and beliefs of individuals and how society thinks, so as to gain greater cultural status for their beliefs and ultimately to change American culture and society through their rationalist Christianity. Appropriators offer many different types of outreach and missions activities, some local and some with a broader reach, all oriented to not leaving any opportunity out—again the emphasis is on a variety of activities to choose from.

All of the different efforts and characteristics of each of these types should be understood as responses to what each sees as the challenges, opportunities, and/or threats to Christianity in and from the larger culture. Their responses may be understood as embracing these challenges and opportunities, or being wary and resistant to them, viewing them as a threat, or even being a retreat from them, back into a structure that provides the answers they believe they need. Regardless, these responses illustrate how much more complex the interaction is between generational identity, one's religious and spiritual quest, and what that means for how different religious commitments might be understood and explained. To suggest that a particular generational identity, whether Baby Boomers, Generation X, Y, or Millennials, can be captured in a single identity and that this will result in a particular religious/spiritual form is a bit too simplistic. Further, we would argue that although the different types we have detailed here are either initiated by or intended to capture the interest and commitment of Post-Boomers, the effects are much broader than that, as evidenced by the multigenerational attraction of each of the efforts in each of these types. In other words, we find both Innovators and Resisters, Appropriators and Reclaimers, appealing to Post-Boomers and Baby Boomers, and in some cases folks older than Boomers, orienting their approach, whether they embrace or resist current cultural trends and the related demands and desires of believers, around issues of visual symbols, ritual and tradition, and involving the whole person, mental, physical, and emotional, in their efforts.

Embodied Spirituality

Taking the different characteristics of the Innovators, Appropriators, Resisters, and Reclaimers together, perhaps the best way to describe these approaches is that they are either embracing, appropriating, or resisting a spirituality centered on experience, lived community, and the body. That is, each of the types we have discussed address these three aspects of spiritual life in a variety of ways, from the Innovators and Reclaimers, who embrace the body, community, and experience, to Appropriators, who seek personal identity, expression, and experience that imitates much that is available in the larger culture, and Resisters, who work hard to deny the body and experience, and seek to create their own sense of community through their insistence on rationality, logic, and cognitive pursuits.

We have seen how Reclaimers and Innovators pursue a spirituality that only makes sense in the context of the religious community and through demonstrating those spiritual commitments in the larger, surrounding community, rather than pursuing an exclusively, or even primarily, individualistic spiritual quest. Similarly, we have seen how Appropriators and Resisters are much more oriented toward an individualistic spirituality, but even they have situated themselves in like-minded communities, with Appropriators located in communities oriented around a consumption identity while Resisters are organized around their opposition to these approaches and then rail against the experiential and body-oriented approach of each of the other types described here.

For two of our types, Innovators and Reclaimers, there is certainly a personal spiritual journey, perhaps even quest, involved, but there is much more to the story than just that. As different as these types are, we find that overall the quest exhibited by these young people is to seek out smaller, more intimate communities of faith so that they can pursue their spiritual journey *within* those communities and directly contribute to the life of those communities, instead of constantly shopping for a better spiritual experience elsewhere. That is, their "journey" is intended to take place within a particular community of faith, not as something they pursue that is separate from their commitment to that community. Further, the spiritual journey is only partly introspective. That is, in addition to the personal desire and effort to grow or develop their spiritual lives, there is also an outward orientation that they understand as being an integral part of their overall spiritual development. Thus we see not only public expressions of their spiritual and emotional states during a worship service, or a gallery exhibit that details a particular spiritual journey, but we see spiritual commitments channeled outward to the surrounding communities through various outreach initiatives.

In all of their spiritual efforts and activities, both personal/introspective and outward/community directed, the spirituality displayed is best understood as taking place in an *embodied* form through visual and physical manifestations of spiritual experience that are practiced in and through a particular religious community. That is, spiritual experience takes place within a body of believers and is only meaningful as it is experienced in that context and as lived out through that body. Although Reclaimers and Innovators each find different contexts for embodied spirituality, Reclaimers looking to history and tradition and Innovators developing combinations of the historical and the (post) modern, they each find it in very similar ways. Reclaimers are drawn to the ritual and symbols of the liturgy, Innovators participate in creating ritual and symbols for their worship services. Each are finding fulfillment in smaller religious communities, as these are viewed as the best places for the commitment and involvement they seek. In each, these young people are not lone seekers; rather, their seeking is embodied in the community.

While Innovators and Reclaimers seek out smaller, more intimate communities, Appropriators seek out the larger, popular venues as the place to pursue their spiritual journey. For them it is clearly about self-expression and identity, primarily through religious consumer goods of one sort or another, each providing a way to simultaneously identify with Christianity and with the larger cultural currents they are drawn to. Appropriators are similar to Innovators and Reclaimers, however, in that they seek an embodied representation of their identity and beliefs, as well as the popular experiential worship that their churches provide and the outreach and missions opportunities that are intended as spiritual fulfillment for them. It is important to note, though, that the outward-oriented activities of Appropriators are such that they don't require any sort of long-term commitment such as we find among the Innovators and to a somewhat lesser extent the Reclaimers.

The lone dissenting voice in the emphasis on embodied spirituality comes from the Resisters, and perhaps appropriately so, in that they largely conceive of themselves as standing against the current of both the "postmodern" developments in the larger culture and how these are coming to be expressed within different Christian communities. Yet their opposition itself can be understood as the exception that proves the rule so to speak, in that through their active resistance to all spiritual developments and activities rooted in the body and in community, they acknowledge the extent to which the embodied approach to spirituality has become almost expected in many Christian churches and ministries. Further, their somewhat contrived attempts at providing an experiential or entertainment component to their otherwise rationalist, almost academic approach to their events suggests both an acknowledgment of the desire for embodiment and experience among the Post-Boomers they seek to attract and how out of touch they really are with this population. For example, a magician, regardless who he may have performed for, and a Malcolm Muggeridge impersonator—in full makeup or not—seem ill-suited to the sensibilities of Post-Boomers, certainly any of those we have interacted with who are instead interested in expressing their Christian faith through various artistic and missions/service types of outreach efforts, whether in their host cities or abroad, rather than the performance/entertainment model.

We would make one additional note here regarding the emphasis on an embodied spirituality among Post-Boomers. Many of the groups that we would include among our Innovators and even many Appropriator churches have been influenced by the "Pentecostalization" of much of Christianity, particularly in terms of breaking down the Cartesian mind-body split. What is particularly important here is that the Pentecostal and Neo-Pentecostal movements have been at the forefront in embodying their faith—through a physical experience of the spirit, healing, and utilizing contemporary musical forms in their worship services—and in giving ministries to the lay people. In a related fashion, this Pentecostalization has also had an effect on our Reclaimers in that many of those that we interviewed came out of a Pentecostal background seeking the history, tradition and stability that the liturgical traditions offer, without giving up the experiential and participatory elements of the expression of their faith. And again, the outliers are the Resisters, who are opposed to all things experiential, so much so that as one Resister suggested, even the Holy Spirit must be controlled as Christians seek its guidance.[2]

Two Examples

To this point, we have emphasized the characteristics of different responses to the same cultural developments and influences, especially as evidenced in the Post-Boomer generation, which could lead one to conclude that there is a certain inevitability to our typology and the different approaches it represents. In this section, however, we would like to highlight two very different organizations that are approaching their Christian commitments in remarkably similar ways, and which have centered their efforts around several of the characteristic needs and desires exhibited by Post-Boomers and that we have identified across each of the types we have been describing, in particular what we have framed as an embodied spirituality. Thus, on the one hand, we provide a snapshot of Saddleback Church in Lake Forest, California, arguably one of the two or three largest and most recognizable churches in the United States, and on the other, the Dream Center in Los Angeles, which is much less well known, but the scope of its different and varied ministries rivals anything Saddleback has developed.

We believe that each of these, despite the fact that one could argue for placing them in one or another part of our typology, actually transcends the typology and provides models for potential future forms of Christianity that tap into the emerging needs and desires of younger generations of Christians, and thus will also have an effect on older generations as well. In this, both Saddleback and Dream Center emphasize a Christian commitment that takes seriously their theological commitments by embodying it both in the community of faith that each is developing and in the way they are turning outward toward the world in terms of serving its needs, both to the individual and the community, both local and global.

Saddleback Church, Lake Forest, California

Saddleback Church is one of the largest churches in the United States, and has most of the characteristics we associate with such a large enterprise, such as a large suburban physical plant complete with a large multipurpose worship center, several additional semi-permanent "pop-out" tents that house different styles of worship, a children's center, an educational wing, an administrative building, and of course acres of parking.

Further, Saddleback has lots of activities and programs that all look pretty much like our Appropriators,' such as over two thousand small-group fellowships and several different choices in the form and type of worship, all meeting simultaneously on Sunday mornings. It also has, as one of our Innovator pastors said somewhat derisively about mega churches, "a staff of thousands," and programming for what seems like every sort of spiritual need niche you could think of, and it provides a "customizable" Christian experience that is in many ways consumer/choice driven. In fact, the church website, a key entry point and resource for Saddleback attendees, encourages this sort of customizability in which the member/attendee can set up a "my Saddleback" account containing certain "personalized Saddleback features," such as worship preferences, which campus of the church they call home, and on and on.

But while Saddleback certainly has these characteristics, they have, particularly since the publication and enormous success of pastor Rick Warren's 2002 book, *The Purpose-Driven Life*, really focused on getting the church and its members looking beyond their own personal development, recovery, spiritual fulfillment, or other similar emphases, and focusing outward to serve a larger vision of Christian belief and life. Most of this is due to Warren's application of his "purpose-driven" principles in his own church, and equally important, to the success of the book, which has allowed and encouraged Warren and his wife to develop a different vision for spiritual development that is directed as much outside of one's individual life as it is in developing one's personal spiritual life. As such, Saddleback can be seen as growing out of, or developing beyond, a relatively simplistic, seeker-oriented, individualistic emphasis that we have framed here as Appropriators and in the process tapping into some of the themes that we have discussed in the previous chapters, in particular the desire and need for people to develop an embodied spirituality in the context of a commitment to the faith community as well as a commitment to developing their spiritual lives beyond simply developing their own inner life.

There are three main characteristics of Saddleback that we see as tapping the emerging emphasis on spiritual embodiment, both in community and in service: first, small groups as the core of the church; second, the "purpose-driven" ideology that encourages service to God and others; and third, the development of the "P.E.A.C.E." plan that institutionalizes their emphasis on serving others. These have all been connected to each other at Saddleback, with the small groups being the central organizing entity at the church in terms of mobilizing the members to participate in the new efforts.

Saddleback's emphasis on small groups is in many ways quite similar to that of most other mega churches, in that due to the sheer size of the church, these are essential for the development of personal relationships among members and to developing a feeling of belonging—community even—that might not be possible without them. Since its founding, Saddleback has emphasized small groups as a way for the church to attract "seekers" and to minister to the growing congregation, and as the locus of personal spiritual growth and development. Yet the small groups at Saddleback are not just affinity groups for personal fulfillment; rather, the emphasis is at least as much on serving the group, working together as a group, and then using the group to minister within the church and in the wider world, both in the local community and in the global arena.

Although it is almost a truism now because of the phenomenal success of the book, the "purpose-driven" approach does permeate the Saddleback culture, from the small groups to the larger congregation. Aside from church-wide programs that happen a couple of times each year, this is not enforced in any sort of top-down manner, but represents guiding principles that are used throughout the different ministries, activities, and small groups in the church throughout the year. At first glance, the

"Purpose-Driven Covenant,"[3] which lays out the purpose
driven ideology in a nutshell, sounds in part somewhat like a
new-agey, personal, spiritual mantra that should be repeated
every day. But upon closer inspection, it is largely framed
around serving others and valuing others over oneself. A few
excerpts will illustrate:

> I will live the rest of my life serving God's purposes with
> God's people on God's planet for God's glory. I will use my
> life to celebrate his presence, cultivate his character, partici-
> pate in his family, demonstrate his love, and communicate
> his word.
>
> Because this life is preparation for the next, I will value
> worship over wealth, "we" over "me," character over com-
> fort, service over status, and people over possessions, posi-
> tion, and pleasures.

> I won't be captivated by culture, manipulated by critics,
> motivated by praise, frustrated by problems, debilitated by
> temptation, or intimidated by the devil. . . . I'll just keep
> moving forward by God's grace. I'm Spirit-led, purpose-
> driven and mission-focused so I cannot be bought, I will not
> be compromised, and I shall not quit until I finish the race.

> To my Lord and Savior Jesus Christ, I say: However,
> Whenever, Wherever, and Whatever you ask me to do, my
> answer in advance is yes! Wherever you lead and whatever
> the cost, I'm ready. Anytime. Anywhere. Anyway.

What is most important about these few excerpts is that
although the individual is acknowledged, the emphasis is not on
the individual pursuing her or his spiritual development in isolation from the community of faith. Rather, the individual com-
mits to both God and to the community first and through that
finds spiritual and emotional fulfillment for herself or himself.
Thus the purpose-driven approach emphasizes an orientation

outward from the self and toward the community of faith and beyond, to serve in the local and global communities.

As a direct result of his *Purpose-Driven* book selling literally millions of copies and the attendant financial windfall and the dramatic increase in his public influence, Rick Warren and his wife, Kay, ultimately rethought their ministry strategies and organized three foundations that were oriented toward both extending the Christian message and alleviating various global social problems. One, "Equipping the Church," focuses on training pastors in developing countries; another, "Acts of Mercy," spearheaded by Kay Warren, focuses on developing programs to help those with HIV/AIDS; and the third is the Global P.E.A.C.E. Plan. They operate in addition to the other programs at Saddleback. However, these major initiatives extend beyond the suburban setting of the church and are intended not only to involve Saddleback members but also to encourage other churches, both in the United States and abroad, to be involved in developing relationships with churches that might be interested in participating in these programs.

Of particular importance for this discussion is the Global P.E.A.C.E. Plan.[4] Briefly, the P.E.A.C.E. plan intends to tackle what Warren describes as the "five global giants," problems that are so overwhelming that "they seem impossible to solve"; they are indeed beyond the capabilities of both the United States and the United Nations to solve.[5] These are, according to Warren, (1) spiritual emptiness for the "billions of people in this world [who] do not know that their life is not an accident," (2) corrupt leadership that is "self-centered" and "self-serving" instead of leadership as modeled by Jesus, where "the leader serves," (3) global poverty, (4) disease, and (5) illiteracy. The way to solve these problems, Warren believes, is essentially to tap into the resources represented by Christians around the world, through networks and partnerships that call both individual Christians and their churches to find ways to serve others both locally and globally. The particular solutions are spelled out through the acronym "P.E.A.C.E." Spiritual emptiness is addressed by "Partnering" with other churches (or "Planting" them where they don't exist); corrupt leadership is solved through "Equipping" servant leaders; "Assist" the poor to solve poverty; "Care" for the sick to address disease; and for illiteracy, "Educate" the next generation.[6]

Saddleback has organized programs, resources, and training around three different levels of working in the P.E.A.C.E. plan: *Personal*, "your personal mission to the people around you," *Local*, "your small group's mission in your region of the world," and *Global*, "our church's mission to the world through small groups." Each of these involves both individuals and groups going out from Saddleback to pursue their own P.E.A.C.E. initiatives, and churches in other parts of the world pursuing their own initiatives, within this general framework. Thus, this reformulating of the Saddleback mission around the purpose driven principles—which are, at least in intent, oriented toward serving others—are given real structure and opportunity through the plan that Warren and his staff have devised.

From our view, these developments and programs are significant for several reasons: First, they are based on the outward-looking principles that seem to drive the church; second, they are only possible on the scale that they are being undertaken because of the resources the church has and through the relationships it has been able to develop because of its status; third, they are primarily lay driven—that is, individuals and small groups make decisions to participate in the programs, within the context that the church provides training and direction; fourth, they are intended to develop relationships with other churches and to help and encourage them to pursue their own P.E.A.C.E. missions (Saddleback personnel provide training; a two-day training program costs only fifty dollars); sixth, Warren envisions every church as a "sending church," meaning that churches around the world develop relationships with other churches to develop different service projects to meet the needs they see, and to encourage this outward looking, service-oriented Christian commitment; seventh, they are social alleviation/justice programs that don't slight theology (in fact, the programs have been developed out of their theological commitments while maintaining these as central parts of their goals); and eighth, they manage to overcome potential "colonization" issues through "partnering" with other churches to work on local problems that are identified by the church in the community being served, not on the needs that Christians from economically advantaged areas might think they can meet by going into another place and dictating what needs to be done.

The Dream Center, Los Angeles, California

While Saddleback Church is situated on the wide parkways in the affluent suburbs of south Orange County, the Dream Center is located two miles from downtown Los Angeles in the Echo Park neighborhood, a tough, largely Hispanic neighborhood of small bungalows and narrow streets. Overlooking the Hollywood Freeway, the Dream Center occupies approximately eight acres at the former Queen of Angels hospital complex, and consists of nine buildings, including the main fourteen-story hospital building. The Dream Center was established in 1996, based on a vision that Tommy Barnett, pastor of First Assembly of God Church in Phoenix, Arizona, had of establishing a church to serve needs of the city of Los Angeles. The story goes that in trying to figure out who would be the ideal person to pastor this new church, one of his church board members suggested that he had the perfect candidate in Barnett's then nineteen-year-old son Matthew.

So at nineteen years of age, Matthew Barnett came to Los Angeles and centered his work at a small, rapidly aging neighborhood church that was essentially coexisting, although not particularly interacting with, residents of the neighborhood, including the many gang members in the area. The younger Barnett developed relationships with the people in the neighborhood by ministering to them and caring for them in terms of both their physical and spiritual needs—by establishing social outreach programs to help with the physical needs of the area and simultaneously working on the spiritual needs as the relationships allowed. As the church grew and developed different ministries and outreach activities intended to meet the immediate needs of those in the neighborhood, it became both a church and a nonprofit outreach organization dedicated to helping inner cities by providing resources to meet both "tangible and spiritual needs."

As a church, the Dream Center offers twelve different church services throughout the week, for all ages, including several different ethnic church services, such as Spanish-language services and Bible study, a Filipino service, and a Japanese service. The services can be pretty rousing times, particularly the ones oriented toward younger people. They have not only their own worship band but their own music label and production facilities. Although still associated with the Assemblies of God, the Dream Center now operates as the outreach arm of the Angelus Temple, a Foursquare Gospel church originally founded and pastored by Aimee Semple McPherson. As a result, it has been able to take advantage of the denominational relationship with the Foursquare denomination in many of their programming efforts, both domestically and internationally, and have developed the church programs into a growing and vibrant congregation that includes many of those to whom it ministers on a daily basis through its outreach programs.

As an outreach organization, the Dream Center is "dedicated to providing the resources and opportunities to help low-income, homeless and underserved individuals and families in the inner city of Los Angeles move toward self-sufficiency through counseling, education, and training."[7] The Dream Center operates over one hundred ministries and outreach programs, including a mobile medical service, several homeless programs, a food distribution program, children's programs that go out to different neighborhoods throughout the city, and an "adopt-a- block" program that currently serves eighty-eight city blocks in Los Angeles, doing yard work, providing food, and providing transportation to Dream Center church services.

In addition to these, the Dream Center operates what it calls a "Discipleship Program," a one-year program in which men and women between the ages of eighteen and fifty-nine who have problems with alcohol, drug abuse, or "other life controlling problems" live on the campus and are active in rehabilitation programs intended to get their lives back on track and turn them into contributing members of society. Those in the discipleship programs also work in different capacities around the site, including in different missions and outreach activities, with the intention of developing different skills and life disciplines, and are ready to share their "testimony" of what the Dream Center has done for them with visitors. This program consistently has 250–300 people living on the Dream Center site.

All of the different programs at the Dream Center operate in large part through various sorts of volunteer help, which, according to Director of Ministry Development Bud Melton, accounts for 92 percent of the Dream Center workforce. There are daily and weekly volunteers who participate in one or another ministry or outreach, as well as opportunities for "short-term missions" experiences for individuals and groups from different churches that range from a few days to a few weeks. Another area of volunteer work is their internship program, in which people commit up to one year to live at the Dream Center and participate in its ministry and outreach programs. One middle-aged man we spoke with told us that he saw the Dream Center on the news in a story dealing with its efforts with people displaced by Hurricane Katrina, and said to his wife, "I've got to go there." He packed up and drove to Los Angeles from Washington State, and has been living at the Dream Center and working there for almost one year. He is one of approximately three hundred volunteers who are living on the campus.

Beyond the different volunteers that come to the Dream Center, the church also operates what it calls "The Master's Commission," which is essentially a one-year Bible school program that also emphasizes the community outreach programs of the Dream Center. Each year, upward of 60–70 college-age men and women come to the Dream Center for this residential education and training program. Bud Melton says that they receive the equivalent of five years of experience in different ministry capacities during their year there, and are thus well equipped to return to their home communities and churches to design and implement similar types of programs to meet the needs of those communities.

Finally, in addition to the original Los Angeles Dream Center, there are 130 Dream Centers in other urban areas across the United States. Each of these has been established by people who wanted to do urban ministry and outreach in their own communities in the same way as the Los Angeles Dream Center, and so they came to Los Angeles to learn the programs and then returned home to set up their own organizations. Each of these operates independently of the Los Angeles center, but they have been trained and can continue to seek, and receive, support from the Los Angeles site. In addition, three Dream Centers have been set up in international settings, in Peru, Uganda, and India. In each, the Dream Center has partnered with local churches to develop organizations and programs to meet the needs in those countries. These are not set up as churches or missionary endeavors, but as social service providers, although they are connected to existing churches and ministries.

Taking all of these activities together, the Dream Center has established itself as a place that is going out into the city and "embodying" its beliefs through its services to the community, and at the same time providing a venue for other Christian believers, both individuals and groups, to participate with them in their service programs. Further, the partnerships that the Dream Center has developed show a similar approach as that at Saddleback Church. That is, they haven't simply decided what programs will or won't work, but have developed programs based on the needs of particular communities, as expressed to them through the different relationships that they have developed with other churches.

Both Saddleback and the Dream Center suggest interesting developments that move beyond the four types we have presented above, while tapping into the primary desires and needs demonstrated by those types. For example, both organizations are models of post- or trans-denominational ministry efforts. The Dream Center is both an Assemblies of God ministry and affiliated with Angelus Temple, a Foursquare Gospel church, but they don't seem to much care about denominations in terms of who participates or volunteers in their programs. Although their history and identity is now with the Foursquare denomination, and they use its resources, especially organizational know-how available to them as they expand their operations in the United States and into other countries, their primary identity is as the Dream Center and the many and varied ministries and outreach programs that it has. This is true as well for Saddleback. Although it is officially Southern Baptist, its main identity is simply Christian and it seems more interested in getting the work done that it has envisioned, and cooperating with like-minded Christians, than in thinking about obscure denominational or otherwise divisive doctrinal issues. Finally, each does have a basic doctrinal/theological commitment that is foundational to their different ministry programs, and their social service/outreach programs develop out of their theological understanding and commitments. They have neglected neither their theological commitments nor their commitment to serving others in their programs.

These two examples each capture important aspects of what we have heard from the different places we have visited and people we have interviewed, but have also moved beyond some of the more contentious issues that have been raised by the different types we have discussed. For example, both have been able to embrace globalization in some sense, both in terms of the diverse and pluralistic culture of the United States and in dealing with issues in the larger world. Through their theology and programs they have been able to argue that as Christian believers they have a responsibility to the broader world, and that they should not just be retreating, or staying in their minds, or remaining individually focused in their pursuit of spiritual development and fulfillment. Further, these broader concerns include a commitment to, and are based on, theology. In other words, theology matters to these churches, but not as a splitting of fine points of doctrine, or a continual chorus of "it's rational" or that "we need to be relevant," but in the sense that their beliefs—their theology—includes *doing* something about issues both local and global, such as poverty, AIDS, education, hunger, homelessness, and other similar problems. Finally, they have been able to utilize cultural currents for larger ends than just individual fulfillment or rationalist navel gazing in the service to their religious ideals. They have figured out not only how to develop these programs, but how to motivate and involve large numbers of fellow Christians in their efforts.

We would like to make one final note here regarding what appear to be preoccupations with each of the types we have discussed, and which are conspicuous by their absence at both the Dream Center and at Saddleback. That is, while each of the types we have discussed have alternately framed their approach, either explicitly or implicitly, in terms of "postmodernism," or "ancient traditions," or "rationalism," or more broadly, the pursuit of an ethic of consumption, however oriented toward spiritual identification it may be, those categories are simply irrelevant in the context of the programs developed by the Dream Center and Saddleback. Nobody we spoke with or heard is thinking in or talking about those categories. Most telling in this, for example, are the testimonies we heard from young people working at the Dream Center as we toured the grounds there. We heard from several young men and women who were barely in their twenties who prior to their coming to the Dream Center were wasting away through their drug and alcohol abuse and gang affiliations, and who report that their lives have literally been saved through the programs at the Dream Center. They are now being "discipled" and trained to be fully functioning, contributing members of a community, and in their community.

What James Smith, the Calvin College philosopher, has written of the emerging church movement, that the very "posture of questioning" that animates much of that movement is in fact a bourgeois privilege that is largely "the province of college-educated middle class America" (James Smith 2003), can in fact be applied to our entire typology. The Resisters enjoy the bourgeois privilege of arguing for reason as the ultimate and only way to know God, Appropriators enjoy the privilege of almost infinite consumer choice as they fashion their individual spiritual identities, Reclaimers enjoy the privilege of seeking out small communities of faith where they can have spiritual direction and belong to a community, and Innovators enjoy the privilege of fashioning a new approach to their lifelong faith commitments. However, in the social reality in which the Dream Center operates, and in the places that Saddleback wants to take its P.E.A.C.E. plan, the necessities of life and death, food, shelter, and clothing, trump the luxury of any of these conversations about postmodernism, rationality, or who has the most ancient Christian tradition. Which is not to say that they don't have their rousing worship services, complete with really good music, drama, video, PowerPoint, and the like, but that they are living in a completely different place than the other kinds of conversations we heard, which, in our view, puts those other conversations in a fairly ephemeral context. In the end, these two organizations represent the possibility of transcending the approaches we identified in our typology, while addressing the desires for an embodied Christian spirituality and commitment.

EXPRESSIVE COMMUNALISM

The emphasis on embodiment and community, whether through using one's body in worship or in living out, or embodying, Christian teachings, suggests that there are many who are seeking a new form of spirituality that goes beyond the individualistic questing that characterizes much of the sociological literature on spirituality. The groups we have been describing, whether embracing or resisting these trends, have shown that there is a new, or perhaps renewed, emphasis on an embodied worship and service, and a desire for seeking, creating, and committing to a particular faith community. It is in the context of these faith communities where one can be both personally fulfilled, and where one can serve others, whether in one's own religious community, or with the homeless in Los Angeles, or with AIDS victims in Africa. We also believe that although much of this new form is driven by and related to Post-Boomer concerns and desires, there is also a significant representation from among older generations as well, who have in many ways become travelers along the trail being blazed by their younger fellow believers.

How then can we make theoretical sense of this new concern with the embodiment of the spiritual that we have found in all four of our types? Max Weber's famous typology of the different forms of asceticism and mysticism (1993), in particular his description of "inner-worldly asceticism," that has characterized the religious impulse of most of western Protestantism since the reformation, and Robert Bellah's 1985 description of "utilitarian individualism" and "expressive individualism," provide a beginning and points of departure.

For Weber, inner-worldly asceticism requires the believer, while seeking the assurance of her or his salvation, to live a rationally ordered life, rejecting "everything that is ethically irrational, esthetic, or dependent upon his own emotional reactions to the world and its institutions" (168). Ascetic Protestantism, according to Weber,

> demanded of the believer, not celibacy, as in the case of the monk, but the avoidance of all erotic pleasure; not poverty, but the elimination of all idle and exploitative enjoyment of unearned wealth and income, and the avoidance of all feudalistic, sensuous ostentation of wealth; not the ascetic death-in-life of the cloister, but an alert, rationally controlled patterning of life, and the avoidance of all surrender to the beauty of the world, to art, or to one's own moods and emotions. The clear and uniform goal of this asceticism was the disciplining and methodical organization of the whole pattern of life. (183)

Thus the believer strives to live her or his life "in the world, but not of the world," so to speak, operating within its constructs and confines, all the while rejecting its various measures of success and sensuous enjoyment and fulfillment, instead focusing on a rationally ordered life and faith.

Robert Bellah and his colleagues present what are essentially the secularized and almost completely individualized outcomes of this emphasis on the rational ordering of life in their description of utilitarian individualism as "a life devoted to the calculating pursuit of one's own material interest," (1985, 33) and expressive individualism as the desire to "cultivate and express the self and explore its vast social and cosmic identities" (1985, 35). The example of the former is Benjamin Franklin, famous for such aphorisms as "a penny saved is a penny earned" and "God helps them who help themselves," while American transcendentalist poet Walt Whitman, famous for poems such as "Song of Myself," is the example of the latter. In each, the emphasis is on an individualism so encompassing that the authors wrote two books worrying about what such an emphasis on individualism in American culture might mean for the future of American society (Bellah et al. 1985; 1991).

The embodied spirituality of the groups we have been describing here cannot be adequately described by any of these three types. In neither their spiritual pursuits nor in the development of their interests and abilities have they rejected their "moods and emotions" or their artistic expression or aesthetic enjoyment, nor have they given up their enjoyment of the "beauty of the world." The dominant characteristic across our types—Resisters notwithstanding—is a desire for a theologically grounded belief that makes sense cognitively combined with nonrational expressive tendencies—they want a faith that makes cognitive sense to them and that is also an expressive, embodied spiritual experience. Indeed, we would argue that Resisters' opposition to the experiential dimension, combined with their attempts to include the same in some of their efforts to attract Post-Boomers, points up the fact that young Christians are searching for a more holistic expression of Christian faith than what a purely cognitive and rational approach can offer.

Similarly, although Post-Boomers certainly pursue individual religious and spiritual experience, they do not seem to be so completely immersed in the forms of individualism identified by Bellah that they have neglected the various communities within which they are active. Rather, the dominant trend of the types

profiled here show an intentional pursuit of artistic expressions
of various sorts, seeking and forming communities, and engaging in different forms of community outreach and involvement.
In other words, pursuing precisely what Bellah worried was
being lost, a commitment to the larger public order. In the cases
described here, whatever the extent of such involvement, it is
motivated by these Post-Boomers' desire to live out what they
see as the imperatives of the Christian faith. This is not to suggest that they have somehow removed themselves from the individualism that pervades American society, rather that their
individual spiritual quest is mediated through the communities
in which they are active and in which they seek membership
and belonging.

Thus, whether it is through the stained glass, icons, and
incense of the liturgical traditions, or the creation of various art-
works intended to express their particular spiritual experience,
or service to others, these only have personal meaning within
the context of the religious community. These young people are
not the spiritual consumers of their parent's generation. Rather,
they are seeking both a deep spiritual experience and a community experience, each of which provides them with meaning in
their lives, and each of which is meaningless without the other.
Further, their community commitments are not necessarily
restricted to just their own religious community, but generally
include social outreach to the surrounding community as a part
of their spiritual commitments. This is certainly truer of some of
the types that we have described in this book than others, but it
does suggest an expansion on the idea of community for at least
some segments of the Post-Boomer generations, and may signal
a new commitment to a larger, more public engagement among
religiously motivated Post-Boomers.

Thus, we believe that we are witnessing the emergence of a
new form of spirituality, what we are calling "Expressive
Communalism," that, although related to the individualistic

forms of spirituality as described above, is also distinct from them. Post-Boomers have embedded their lives in spiritual communities in which their desire and need for both expressive/experiential activities, whether through art, music, or service-oriented activities, and for a close-knit, physical community and communion with others are met. These young people are seeking out different forms of spirituality in response to the shortcomings they see as inherent in these other forms. They are seeking to develop a balance for individualism and rational asceticism through religious experience and spiritual meaning in an embodied faith.

So what does Expressive Communalism as a new type of spirituality mean for the futures of our Innovators, Reclaimers, Appropriators and Resisters? Will each type, as we have described them, continue as they are into the future, or will they change from their current forms or perhaps even cease to exist at some point? Although social forecasting is always fraught with danger, we would like to suggest some possible outcomes for these different expressions of Christianity within the context of the emphasis on an embodied faith—the Expressive Communalism that we are observing among Post-Boomers.

As we noted earlier, our typology is an abstraction and is useful for both analysis by students of religion and perhaps for self-reflection by different churches and ministries. Thus, our claims and predictions here are related to our types in their "pure" form, not to any particular church or ministry. However, to the extent that churches and ministries can identify themselves within our typology, including what we are arguing is a new or emerging type more descriptive of broad segments of Christianity, they may be able to engage in a bit of self-analysis through our reflections here.

First, we would suggest that given the emphasis on embodiment, whether embracing and seeking it or resisting it, those churches and ministries that are able to capture the "embodied imagination" of young Christians such as we have been describing in this book are more likely to be able to ensure for themselves a vibrant future. Second, we believe that those churches and ministries that are able to engage Post-Boomers at what we constantly heard framed as the "organic" level, that is, where the emphasis is on a participatory approach to church and ministry from the grass roots, or from the members upward into the group, whether that is through small churches or small groups, rather than a top-down program development model, will be more successful in the long run. In this, we have in mind what theologian Alister McGrath has called the "organic theologian" (2002). For McGrath, the organic theologian is one who, unlike the stuffy and authority-laden academic theologian (which McGrath suggests has completely lost touch with Christian practice in the daily life of the church), understands the importance and role of popular culture in the shaping of ideas and the communication of values. Thus, the organic theologian is "an activist, a popularizer—someone who sees his task as supportive and systematic within the community of faith, and as evangelistic and apologetic outside the community" (2002, 151). McGrath concludes that if "Christianity is to survive and flourish, it needs organic theologians, not well-intentioned yet tunnel-visioned students of Richard Hooker or Thomas Aquinas, who know their ideas backwards, yet can neither critique nor apply them, nor even see the need to do so" (2002, 152–53).

As regards our four different types, we would expect that other than the mass appeal of the Appropriators, Innovators have the greatest opportunity to be successful in the long run, although they will always be fighting the threat of the routinization of their structures. That is, it is extremely difficult to be continually innovating and to keep the creative fires burning. These groups would seem to be the most prone to becoming either big and successful, thus necessitating an ever greater emphasis on institution building and maintenance—precisely what we have heard them say they don't want to do—or of simply burning out and ceasing to exist. However, we believe that their emphasis on "organic" program building and a more democratized leadership structure, à la McGrath's organic theologian, makes for a better fit with the cultural sensibilities of Post-Boomers.

Reclaimers, we believe, will always make up a small segment of the Christian community, owing primarily to the high demands of their newly found religious traditions, most of which they place on themselves. As most Reclaimers are converts from evangelicalism or from lapsed faith commitments, it seems likely that this will be a way station for several years until they ultimately find less demanding forms of the various liturgical traditions. We would expect that their emphasis on the embodied nature of the liturgical traditions, in particular the "smells and the bells," will remain; however, the particular congregations into which they may move will likely be much less demanding in terms of their daily participation and their often self-imposed spiritual regimens. Reclaimers seem to not be interested at all in any sort of democratized authority system or the development of organic structures, choosing instead the different liturgical traditions because of the history and authority those traditions provide for their lives. As they move out of the Reclaimer way station, this will likely be one reason, to reclaim some of their own authority in their spiritual lives.

Appropriators, on the other hand, will always attract the masses, as they have proven to be so successful at simultaneously providing a sort of "Christianity lite" entertainment model and making their congregants feel good about their spiritual lives and their participation in these churches and ministries. That is, the demands are quite low, unless one really chooses to participate more deeply in the life of the congregation, yet the benefits can be quite high for simply showing up to church or an event in which everyone basks in the collective effervescence of their shared identity—all the while enjoying some excellent entertainment. And this, it seems, is its own form of organic theologian model, in that while the authority lies at the grass roots, it is located in the individual who chooses, or not, to be involved in one way or another in the programs in a particular congregation. The difference is that the individual is responsible to herself or himself while utilizing, and in fact being dependent on, the available community resources to meet their personal spiritual and psychological needs.

Finally, Resisters are simply fighting a losing battle. Culture has left them behind, and despite their impressive ability to adapt new technologies to aid in their resistance strategies, the forces against which they are aligned are simply overwhelming, in that the emphasis on embodiment and experience is everywhere in culture. To be left arguing for a rational, cognitive approach to Christian belief when, on the one hand, one can be entertained in church, or on the other, one can put one's faith into practical efforts that have been developed out of legitimate concerns that are grounded in the community needs, seems to be an over-whelming task even in the small world they inhabit. Further, their authoritative and expert system approach seems at odds with the way that knowledge and authority has been democra-tized over the last twenty to thirty years. Thus, to attract a Post-Boomer hearing over the long haul, Resisters face the challenge that they would need to give up some of their authority and expert system status to laypersons, which it appears they are loathe to do in any real way, as they are constantly reminding their followers that they are the only legitimate authority in reli-gious and spiritual matters. Ultimately, it is difficult to conceive of a necessary role for Resisters other than one that they are able to convince Christian believers that they already have—the last of the rationalist prophets. To the extent that they are successful in convincing Christians of their expert status, and thus their necessity, they will be more successful.

In the end, of course, time will tell the accuracy of our predictions. Who knows, as Max Weber hinted in his classic work, *The Protestant Ethic and the Spirit of Capitalism*, perhaps "new prophets will arise or there will be a great rebirth of old ideas and ideals," and the typology we have developed and described here will give way to entirely new ways of approaching and living out religious beliefs.

Notes

CHAPTER 2   INNOVATORS

1. This does not seem to be limited to conservative congregations. All Saints Episcopal Church in Pasadena, a liberal standard-bearer, has started a foot-washing service, and it has had a transformative effect on the parishioners there, largely for the same reasons—the embodiment and physicality of the act of serving one another.
2. See chapter three, "Appropriators," and chapter four, "Resisters."
3. http://emergentvillage.com/Site/Explore/EmergentStory/index.htm (accessed November 6, 2006)
4. Soularize ran for six years, from 1999 to 2005, took a break in 2006, and resumed in 2007.
5. http://theooze.com/soularize/events.cfm (accessed November 1, 2005).
6. It is interesting to note here that Dallas Willard is also a favorite scholar of many that we have framed here as Resisters, especially J. P. Moreland, Douglas Geivett, and others who were students of his at the University of Southern California. See chapter four, "Resisters," for more on Moreland, Geivett, and company. Note as well that N. T. Wright was a participant in a Resister-sponsored conference in November 2006, although he was relegated to a one-hour "Workshop" session—one among five choices for conference participants.
7. http://brianmclaren.net (accessed August 31, 2006).
8. Emergent/C, October 5, 2005.
9. http://apostleschurch.org (accessed August 31, 2006).
10. http://www.symbollife.com (accessed June 28, 2007).

CHAPTER 3   APPROPRIATORS

Epigraph: They Will Know Us by Our T-Shirts blog, maintained by "Ben," of Portland, Oregon, who was reflecting on his job as an employee of a Christian retail store. What caught our eye was his first entry, dated July 13, 2004:

> The first day of work is always fun. You learn the lay of the land, meet new people and try to figure out if you've just

made the biggest mistake of your life. . . . I think my favorite thing of the day was a kids t-shirt. Imagine the Mt. Dew logo, but instead [of] mentioning soda it reads, "Jesus: He Died For You." Do you get it? It sounds like "Do the Dew." Oh my freaking gosh, that is so cool. Move over Billy Graham; this t-shirt will save millions of angry suburban teens from their sins. . . . What have I gotten myself into? [http://christian-retail.blogspot.com (accessed October 2, 2006)]

1. Harvest Crusades have expanded their program over the last few years, holding similar crusades in San Jose, California, and Christchurch, New Zealand (2006), Newcastle, NSW, Australia, and Augusta, Georgia (2005), and Honolulu, Hawaii (2004). The annual Anaheim crusade remains the largest.

2. The Harvest Crusade website (http://harvest.org/crusades) also gives the number of people watching the crusade on the Internet—over ten thousand were reported as watching on the night we visited in 2005.

3. For a description of C28, see below in the "Patterns" section.

4. This seems to be a bit of a trend among Christian groups, in an apparent attempt to present themselves as culturally aware and somewhat edgy. In addition to Kutless, Ryan Dobson, son of Focus on the Family's James Dobson, has a "skate ministry" called "Kor," which means "core." Thus, as near as we can tell, the "K" references the more edgy representations in popular culture, such as the punk/hard-core band Korn—another example of appropriation of popular cultural symbols.

5. We attended in 2005 and 2006, and by 2006 the aggressive connection—even the branding of the event as "Harvest—Greg Laurie"—had been toned down to Harvest 06 and, in smaller type, "With Greg Laurie."

6. At the time of the 2006 Harvest Crusade, so far as we could find out, this movie had not been released, and it was not advertised at the 2006 crusade.

7. These are actual names of different motocross "tricks," although not necessarily performed in that combination.

8. http://www.harvest.org/church/events/sun/day7 (accessed October 1, 2006).

9. See http://www.visionforum.com/booksandmedia/productdetail.aspx?productid=66530&categoryid=159 (accessed October 1, 2006).

10. http://www.imdb.com/title/tt0174163 (accessed November 1, 2006).

11. Although these were not our only church visits, during one particularly instructive weekend we visited four churches in southern California: Mariners Church in Irvine, Rock Harbor in Costa Mesa, The Crossing, also in Costa Mesa (all located within six miles of one another), and Harvest Fellowship in Riverside.

12. For example, the median income in Irvine and neighboring Newport Beach, both cities in which Mariners has been located, is $97,592 and $125,000 respectively, and the median home price is $640,000 in Irvine and $1,400,000 in Newport Beach. By comparison, the median income in Riverside is $53,368 and the median home price is $380,000. See http://money.cnn.com/magazines/moneymag/bplive/2006/snapshots/PL0636770.html (accessed October 5, 2006) for statistics for Irvine; http://money.cnn.com/magazines/moneymag/bplive/2006/snapshots/PL0651182.html (accessed October 5, 2006) for statistics for Newport Beach; and for statistics for Riverside, see http://money.cnn.com/magazines/moneymag/bplive/2006/snapshots/PL0662000.html (accessed October 5, 2006).

13. http://www.harvest.org/church/events/sun/day7 (accessed October 1, 2006).

14. Our thanks to LaDawn Prieto for this term.

15. C28 operates seven stores owned by Barreto, all in southern California, and three franchised stores, two in northern California and one in Florida. Unless otherwise noted, information about C28 is from their website, www.c28.com (accessed October 16, 2006).

16. http://www.c28.com/message.asp (accessed June 24, 2007). This number is up from the 5,411 shown on the website when we accessed it on October 16, 2006.

17. "Fearing Loss of Teenagers, Evangelicals Turn Up the Fire," *New York Times*, October 6, 2006, section A, page 1, column 3.

18. http://www.marinersglobal.org/fa/index.html (accessed December 30, 2006).

19. See http://www.gointernational.tv/home/index.php?option=com_content&task=view&id=102&Itemid (accessed June 24, 2007).

20. Dobson runs his own skateboard ministry, Kor Ministries, but looking at his website (http://korministries.com [accessed February 24, 2007]), it appears that he is spending much more time talking about himself, his wife, his baby, his dog, and his hunting trips with his father than he is anything else. Although his name appears in many of these types of ministry efforts, usually as a "guest speaker," it is not exactly clear what it is he may be talking about.

CHAPTER 4   RESISTERS

Epigraph: Douglas Groothuis, "Outthinking the World for Christ: The Mission of Denver Seminary's Philosophy of Religion Program" (May 12, 2003), http://www.ivpress.com/groothuis/doug/archives/000118.php (accessed August 24, 2006).

1. Webber also shows up in chapter five, because of his accounts of his and others' earlier faith journeys to the Episcopal Church, many themes of which are also appealing to those in the emerging church.

2. Campus Crusade for Christ was founded in 1951 by Bill Bright, to evangelize college campuses in the United States. "The Four Spiritual Laws" was a small fifteen-page tract that was used in this effort. It is still in print in several languages, and also available online at http://www.campuscrusade.com/fourlawseng.htm (accessed September 9, 2006).

3. Carl F. H. Henry, *God, Revelation, and Authority*, 6 vols. (Waco, Tex.: Word Books, 1976–1983).

4. Machen, despite having died in 1937, has a significant presence on the Internet, with most sites praising his stance against modernist Christianity and citing him as an example for current Christian practice, in particular taking an oppositional stance toward post-modernism. We would categorize virtually all of these sites as being Resister oriented.

5. http://ses.edu/about_mission_and_purpose.htm (accessed September 9, 2006).

6. http://boundless.org (accessed September 10, 2006); http://trueu.org (accessed September 10, 2006).

7. http://leaderu.org (accessed September 10, 2006); http://beyond-belief.com/home.spl (accessed September 10, 2006).

8. For example, http://albertmohler.com (accessed September 10, 2006); http://www.ivpress.com/groothuis/doug (accessed September 11, 2006); http://francisbeckwith.com (accessed September 11, 2006); http://scriptoriumdaily.com (accessed September 11, 2006).

9. For example, http://ateam.blogware.com/blog (accessed September 11, 2006); http://frankpastore.com (accessed September 11, 2006); http://scotswahey.blogspot.com (accessed September 11, 2006); sliceoflaodicea.com (accessed September 11, 2006).

10. For example, str.org/site/PageServer; http://arn.org (accessed June 23, 2007); http://www.worldviewweekend.com/secure/cwnetwork/index.php (accessed September 11, 2006); http://www.apologetics.com/default.jsp (accessed September 11, 2006); http://str.typepad.com/weblog (accessed September 11, 2006).

11. For example, http://www.salvomag.com (accessed September 13, 2006); http://www.cruxproject.org (accessed September 13, 2006).

12. Colson seems to have two personae: one, a compassionate leader and founder of a prison ministry; the other, a rabid right-wing radio and magazine commentator.

13. http://breakpoint.org (accessed September 9, 2006).

14. http://pearceyreport.com/archives/2006/01/j_richard_pearc_1.php (accessed September 9, 2006).

15. We interviewed, and attempted to interview, several Resisters with the following results: after two interviews, we were told we could not use the interviews, nor could we use "their image in any way" in our study; following those interviews, we were essentially stonewalled in our attempts to set up further interviews, albeit in a

fairly passive-aggressive manner. The individuals we approached sounded willing and even excited to, as one person said, "have a dialogue," but we were ultimately unsuccessful in our repeated attempts to set up interviews. Further, owing to Resisters' insistence on the written word and rational argumentation, it makes sense to use their writings as a central piece of our evidence, as this is where their rational argumentational skills should be most evident.

16. Douglas Groothuis, "Outhinking the World for Christ."
17. "The Wedge," Discovery Institute, Center for the Renewal of Science and Culture (no date), ten-page paper (available online at http://www.seattleweekly.com/2006–02–01/news/the-wedge.php [accessed August 19, 2006]). See also Johnson's *The Wedge of Truth: Splitting the Foundations of Naturalism*. According to the Discovery Institute, the Wedge document was an "early fund-raising proposal for Discovery Institute's Center for the Renewal of Science and Culture" (http://www.discovery.org/scripts/viewDB/filesDB-download.php?id=349 [accessed June 23, 2007]).
18. *Los Angeles Times*, March 25, 2001, Section A, p. 1.
19. See chapter two, "Innovators," for our description of this movement.
20. Interestingly, we were accused of being "postmodernists" by some Resisters when we mounted an art gallery installation in February 2003 based on this research that laid out the typology we are describing here without making any rank ordering in terms of "good" or "bad" for Christianity—which of course was not, and could not, be our intent
21. We are interested here in their arguments related to culture and not the scientific merits of intelligent design. For recent treatments of the scientific claims of intelligent design, see, for example, Ayala (2006), Shanks (2004), Forrest and Gross (2004), and Young and Edis (2004).
22. http://biola.edu/academics/torrey/about/Reynolds.cfm (accessed June 29, 2006).
23. John Mark Reynolds address to prospective students, March 31, 2001.
24. Pastore won forty-eight games and lost fifty-eight in an eight-year career (1979–1986) with the Cincinnati Reds and the Minnesota Twins (http://www.baseball-reference.com/p/pastofr01.shtml [accessed September 8, 2006]). He still relies on this athletic, competitive identity on his radio show, although now he centers it on ridiculing what he sees as inferior ideas—and those who claim them—from his politically right-wing perspective, albeit with a Christian gloss.
25. Quoted in the April 9, 2007, edition of the *Lakeland [Florida] Ledger*, http://www.theledger.com/apps/pbcs.dll/article?AID=/2007040/NEWS/704090363/1039 (accessed April 9, 2007).

26. For example, the blog sponsored by Stand to Reason Ministries lists 294 mentions of some combination of this phrase in posts dated from 2005 through March 2007 (http://str.typepad.com/weblog [accessed March 5, 2007]).

27. In all of the sources we read, we found only one citation to a specific publication of a postmodern theorist, rather than alluding to a theorist, and that was to a selection out of Lyotard's *The Postmodern Condition*, published in an edited text/reader.

CHAPTER 5   RECLAIMERS

1. We have masked the name and exact location of this church.

2. We also visited a Messianic Jewish congregation, and found that a similar emphasis on finding the most authentic/ancient/true form of Christianity was the Gentile converts' main motivation for converting to Messianic Judaism. When we asked about the Gentile converts, the congregational leader, himself an ethnic Jew, pointed out that it was mostly the Gentile converts who were wearing the prayer shawls and davening during the service, and who tended to try to, as he put it, "out-Jew the Jews" in their embracing of the rituals and experiences available in the Jewish tradition. On this theme, see also Shoshanah Feher (1998), in particular her discussion of Gentile converts.

3. On several occasions, both while visiting different churches and while interviewing Reclaimers, we were asked whether we would consider "becoming" Orthodox, or Episcopalian, etc. Each time the question seemed really to be a suggestion similar to that made by the Orthodox Father we described at the beginning of this chapter, that we needed to become involved in a church tradition that was more completely developed, more true, and/or unaffected by the incursions of culture.

4. A quick Google search on "spiritual formation" netted over 12 million hits, with several Christian traditions and parachurch organizations, as well as several evangelical seminary programs, listed on the first several pages.

CHAPTER 6   CONCLUSION

1. Moreland (1997) quotes Postman (1985, 9) in an epigraph to his opening chapter as part of his argument for his rationalist approach to Christianity. Postman is commenting on Mosaic Law and says, "The God of the Jews was to exist in the Word and through the Word, an unprecedented conception requiring the highest order of abstract thinking." Moreland fails to mention what, for example, Innovators and Reclaimers explicitly emphasize, that as recorded in the New Testament Gospel of John, the "Word became flesh and

lived among us" (John 1:14), suggesting that the "Word" is more than just an idea or either the result or cause or expression of logical, rational thinking.

2. For a history of Pentecostalism, see Anderson 2004; for recent developments in global Pentecostalism, see Miller and Yamamori 2007.

3. http://saddleback.com/flash/covenant.html (accessed September 25, 2006).

4. Although the P.E.A.C.E. Plan and the HIV/AIDS Initiative are organized separately from each other, we focus our discussion on the P.E.A.C.E. plan because in many ways the actions that it encourages include much that the HIV/AIDS Initiative intends. For a full description of each of these, see the Saddleback websites: saddleback.org and saddlebackfamily.com.

5. Transcript, "Myths of the Modern Mega-Church," Pew Forum on Religion and Public Life, May 23, 2005, available at http://pewforum.org/events/index.php?EventID=80 (accessed April 27, 2007).

6. Pew Forum Transcript; P.E.A.C.E. Plan brochure, Saddleback Church; http://saddlebackfamily.com/peace (accessed September 17, 2006). Note that P.E.A.C.E. is an acronym: P (Partner/Plant churches) E (Equip servant leaders), A (Assist the poor), C (Care for the sick), E (Educate the next generation).

7. "Dream Center Ministry Upclose," n.d., brochure handout available from The Dream Center, 2301 Bellevue Avenue, Los Angeles, CA 90026.

References

Anderson, Allan. 2004. *An Introduction to Pentecostalism: Global Charismatic Christianity.* Cambridge: Cambridge Univ. Press.

Ayala, Francisco Jose. 2006. *Darwin and Intelligent Design.* Minneapolis: Fortress Press.

Bagdikian, Ben H. 2000. *The Media Monopoly.* Boston: Beacon Press.

Baker, Jonny, and Doug Gay. 2003. *Alternative Worship.* London: SPCK.

Beckerman, Gal. 2004. "Why Don't Journalists Get Religion? A Tenuous Bridge to Believers." *Columbia Journalism Review,* May/June 2004, 26–30.

Beckwith, Francis J. 2004. "Introduction." In *To Everyone an Answer: A Case for the Christian Worldview,* ed. Francis J. Beckwith, William Lane Craig, and J. P. Moreland. Downers Grove, Ill.: InterVarsity Press.

Bellah, Robert N., Richard Madsen, William M. Sullivan, Ann Swidler, and Steven M. Tipton. 1985. *Habits of the Heart: Individualism and Commitment in American Life.* Berkeley and Los Angeles: Univ. of California Press.

———. 1991. *The Good Society.* New York: Knopf.

Belzer, Tobin, Richard Flory, Brie Loskota, and Nadia Roumani. 2006. "Congregations That Get It: Understanding Religious Identities in the Next Generation." In *Passing on the Faith: Transforming Traditions for the Next Generation of Jews, Christians, and Muslims,* ed. James L. Heft, S.M. New York: Fordham Univ. Press.

Brand, Chad Owen. 2004. "Defining Evangelicalism." Chapter 11 in *Reclaiming the Center: Confronting Evangelical Accommodation in Postmodern Times,* ed. Millard J. Erickson, Paul Kjoss Helseth, and Justin Taylor. Wheaton, Ill.: Crossway Books.

Burke, Spencer. 2003. "From the Third Floor to the Garage." Chapter 1 in *Stories of Emergence: Moving from Absolute to Authentic,* ed. Mike Yaconelli. Grand Rapids, Mich.: Zondervan/Emergent/YS Books.

Burnett, Ron. 2005. *How Images Think.* Cambridge, Mass.: MIT Press.

Carroll, Colleen. 2002. *The New Faithful: Why Young Adults Are Embracing Christian Orthodoxy.* Chicago: Loyola Press.

Carroll, Jackson W., and Wade Clark Roof. 2002. *Bridging Divided Worlds: Generational Cultures in Congregations.* San Francisco: Jossey-Bass.

Carson, D. A. 2004. "Domesticating the Gospel: A Review of Stanley Grenz's Renewing the Center." Chapter 2 in *Reclaiming the Center: Confronting Evangelical Accommodation in Postmodern Times*, ed. Millard J. Erickson, Paul Kjoss Helseth, and Justin Taylor. Wheaton, Ill.: Crossway Books.

———. 2005. *Becoming Conversant with the Emerging Church: Understanding a Movement and Its Implications*. Grand Rapids, Mich.: Zondervan.

Cimino, Richard P. 1997. *Against the Stream: The Adoption of Traditional Christian Faiths by Young Adults*. Lanham, Md.: Univ. Press of America.

Cimino, Richard, and Don Lattin. 1998. *Shopping for Faith: American Religion in the New Millennium*. San Francisco: Jossey-Bass.

Coupland, Douglas. 1991. *Generation X: Tales for an Accelerated Culture*. New York: St. Martin's Press.

Craig, William Lane. 1994. *Reasonable Faith: Christian Truth and Apologetics*, rev. ed. Wheaton, Ill.: Crossway Books.

———. 2004. "Introduction" to "Part 1: Faith, Reason and the Necessity of Apologetics." In *To Everyone an Answer: A Case for the Christian Worldview*, ed. Francis J. Beckwith, William Lane Craig, and J. P. Moreland. Downers Grove, Ill.: InterVarsity Press.

Cremeens, Fr. Timothy. 1992. "Back to Pentecost." Chapter 10 in *Coming Home: Why Protestant Clergy Are Becoming Orthodox*, ed. Peter Gillquist. Ben Lomand, Calif.: Conciliar Press.

Dawkins, Richard. 2006. *The God Delusion*. New York: Houghton Mifflin.

DeWeese, Garrett J. 2002. "Postmodern Ministry?" *Sundoulos* (fall): 6–8.

———. 2005. "Review of *The Church in Emerging Culture: Five Perspectives*, ed. Leonard Sweet." *Christian Education Journal*, series 3, vol. 2, no. 2, 420–26.

Erickson, Millard J. 2004. "On Flying in the Theological Fog." Chapter 13 in *Reclaiming the Center: Confronting Evangelical Accommodation in Postmodern Times*, ed. Millard J. Erickson, Paul Kjoss Helseth, and Justin Taylor. Wheaton, Ill.: Crossway Books.

Feher, Shoshanah. 1998. *Passing Over Easter: Constructing Boundaries of Messianic Judaism*. Walnut Creek, Calif.: AltaMira Press.

Florida, Richard. 2002. *The Rise of the Creative Class*. New York: Basic Books.

Flory, Richard W., and Donald E. Miller, eds. 2000. *GenX Religion*. New York: Routledge.

Forrest, Barbara, and Paul R. Gross. 2004. *Creationism's Trojan Horse: The Wedge of Intelligent Design*. Oxford Univ. Press.

Foster, Richard J. 1998. *The Celebration of Discipline: The Path to Spiritual Growth*. [San Francisco]: HarperSanFrancisco.

Fuller, Robert C. 2001. *Spiritual But Not Religious: Understanding Unchurched America*. New York: Oxford Univ. Press.

Gallatin, Matthew. 2002. *Thirsting for God in a Land of Shallow Wells*. Ben Lomand, Calif.: Conciliar Press.

Geivett, R. Douglas. 2005. "Is God a Story? Postmodernity and the Task of Theology." Chapter 1 in *Christianity and the Postmodern Turn*, ed. Myron B. Penner. Grand Rapids, Mich.: Brazos Press.

————. 2006. "What Should Christians Know about Brian McLaren's 'Generous Orthodoxy'?" *Biola Connections* (winter): 7.

Giggie, John Michael, and Diane Winston. 2002. *Faith in the Market: Religion and the Rise of Urban Commercial Culture*. New Brunswick, N.J., and London: Rutgers Univ. Press.

Gilbert, James. 1997. *Redeeming Culture: American Religion in an Age of Science*. Chicago: Univ. of Chicago Press.

Gillquist, Peter E. 1992 [1989]. *Becoming Orthodox: A Journey to the Ancient Christian Faith*. Ben Lomand, Calif.: Conciliar Press.

Gillquist, Peter E., ed. 1995 [1992]. *Coming Home: Why Protestant Clergy Are Becoming Orthodox*. Ben Lomand, Calif.: Conciliar Press.

Grenz, Stanley. 1996. *A Primer on Postmodernism*. Grand Rapids, Mich.: Eerdmans.

Groothuis, Douglas. "Outthinking the World for Christ: The Mission of Denver Seminary's Philosophy of Religion Program." May 12, 2003. http://www.ivpress.com/groothuis/doug/archives/000118.php (accessed August 24, 2006).

———— 2000. *Truth Decay: Defending Christianity Against the Challenges of Postmodernism*. Downers Grove, Ill.: InterVarsity Press.

————. 2004a. "Facing the Challenge of Postmodernism." Chapter 14 in *To Everyone an Answer: A Case for the Christian Worldview*, ed. Francis J. Beckwith, William Lane Craig, and J. P. Moreland. Downers Grove, Ill.: InterVarsity Press.

————. 2004b. "Truth Defined and Defended." Chapter 3 in *Reclaiming the Center: Confronting Evangelical Accommodation in Postmodern Times*, ed. Millard J. Erickson, Paul Kjoss Helseth, and Justin Taylor. Wheaton, Ill.: Crossway Books.

Hansen, Mark B. N. 2004. *New Philosophy for New Media*. Cambridge, Mass.: MIT Press.

Harris, Sam. 2005. *The End of Faith*. New York: Free Press.

————. 2006. *Letter to a Christian Nation*. New York: Knopf.

Hauerwas, Stanley. 1991. *After Christendom?* Nashville: Abingdon Press.

————. 2000. *A Better Hope: Resources for a Church Confronting Capitalism, Democracy, and Postmodernity*. Grand Rapids, Mich.: Brazos Press.

Henry, Carl F. H. 1947. *The Uneasy Conscience of Modern Fundamentalism*. Grand Rapids, Mich.: Eerdmans.

―――. 1976–1983. *God, Revelation, and Authority.* 6 vols. Waco, Tex.: Word Books.

Howe, Neil, and William Strauss. 2000. *Millennials Rising: The Next Great Generation.* New York: Vintage Books.

Hunter, James Davison. 1987. *Evangelicalism: The Coming Generation.* Chicago: Univ. of Chicago Press.

Johnson, Phillip E. 1995. *Reason in the Balance: The Case Against Naturalism in Science, Law, and Education.* Downers Grove, Ill.: InterVarsity Press.

―――. 2002. *The Wedge of Truth: Splitting the Foundations of Naturalism.* Downers Grove, Ill.: InterVarsity Press.

―――. 2007. "Harvard's End." In *Touchstone: A Journal of Mere Christianity,* January/February. http://www.touchstonemag.com/archives/article.php?id=20-01-014-c (accessed February 5, 2007).

Kellner, Douglas. 1995. *Media Culture: Cultural Studies, Identity and Politics Between the Modern and the Postmodern.* New York: Routledge.

Kilde, Jeanne Halgren. 2002. *When Church Became Theatre: The Transformation of Evangelical Architecture and Worship in Nineteenth-Century America.* New York: Oxford Univ. Press.

Lucas, Phillip Charles. 2003. "Enfants Terribles: The Challenge of Sectarian Converts to Ethnic Orthodox Churches in the United States." *Nova Religio* 7, no. 2, 5–23.

Lyotard, Jean-François. 1984. *The Postmodern Condition: A Report on Knowledge.* Minneapolis: Univ. of Minnesota Press.

Mannheim, Karl. 1952. "The Problem of Generations." Chapter 7 in *Essays on the Sociology of Knowledge.* London: Routledge and Kegan Paul.

Manovich, Lev. 2002. *The Language of the New Media.* Cambridge, Mass.: MIT Press.

Marsden, George. 1980. *Fundamentalism and American Culture.* New York and Oxford: Oxford Univ. Press.

Mathewes-Green, Frederica. 1997. *Facing East: A Pilgrim's Journey into the Mysteries of Orthodoxy.* New York and San Francisco: HarperSanFrancisco.

―――. 2001. *The Illumined Heart: The Ancient Christian Path of Transformation.* Brewster, Mass.: Paraclete Press.

McDannell, Colleen. 1998. *Material Christianity: Religion and Popular Culture in America.* New Haven: Yale Univ. Press.

McGrath, Alister. 2002. *The Future of Christianity.* Oxford: Blackwell Publishers.

McLaren, Brian. 1999. *Finding Faith: A Self-Discovery Guide for Your Spiritual Quest.* Grand Rapids, Mich.: Zondervan.

―――. 2000 [1998]. *The Church on the Other Side: Doing Ministry in the Postmodern Matrix.* Grand Rapids, Mich.: Zondervan.

————. 2001. *A New Kind of Christian: A Tale of Two Friends on a Spiritual Journey*. San Francisco: Jossey-Bass.

————. 2002. *More Ready than You Realize: Evangelism as Dance in the Postmodern Matrix*. Grand Rapids, Mich.: Zondervan.

————. 2004. *A Generous Orthodoxy*. Grand Rapids, Mich.: Zondervan/Emergent/YS Books.

Miller, Donald. 2003. *Blue Like Jazz: Nonreligious Thoughts on Christian Spirituality*. Nashville: Thomas Nelson Publishers.

————. 2004. *Searching For God Knows What*. Nashville: Thomas Nelson Publishers.

Miller, Donald E. 1997. *Reinventing American Protestantism: Christianity in the New Millennium*. Berkeley and Los Angeles: Univ. of California Press.

Miller, Donald E., and Tetsunao Yamamori. 2007. *Global Pentecostalism: The New Face of Christian Social Engagement*. Berkeley and Los Angeles: Univ. of California Press.

Moore, R. Laurence. 1994. *Selling God: American Religion in the Marketplace of Culture*. New York: Oxford Univ. Press.

Moreland, J. P. 1993. "Introduction." In *Christian Perspectives on Being Human: A Multidisciplinary Approach to Integration*, ed. J. P. Moreland and David M. Ciocchi. Grand Rapids, Mich.: Baker Books.

————. 1994. "Introduction." In *The Creation Hypothesis: Scientific Evidence for an Intelligent Designer*. Downers Grove, Ill: InterVarsity Press.

————. 1997. *Love Your God with All Your Mind: The Role of Reason in the Life of the Soul*. Colorado Springs, Colo.: Navpress.

Moreland, J. P., and William Lane Craig. 2003. *Philosophical Foundations for a Christian Worldview*. Downers Grove, Ill: InterVarsity Press.

Moreland, J. P., and Garrett DeWeese. 2004. "The Premature Report of Foundationalism's Demise." Chapter 4 in *Reclaiming the Center: Confronting Evangelical Accommodation in Postmodern Times*, ed. Millard J. Erickson, Paul Kjoss Helseth, and Justin Taylor. Wheaton, Ill: Crossway Books.

Newbigin, Lesslie. 1989. *The Gospel in a Pluralist Society*. Grand Rapids, Mich.: Eerdmans.

Niebuhr, H. Richard. 2001 [1951]. *Christ and Culture*. San Francisco: HarperSanFrancisco.

Oden, Thomas C. 2003. *The Rebirth of Orthodoxy: Signs of New Life in Christianity*. New York and San Francisco: HarperSanFrancisco.

Oldenburg, Ray. 1999. *The Great Good Place: Cafes, Coffee Shops, Bookstores, Bars, Hair Salons, and other Hangouts at the Heart of a Community*. New York: Marlowe.

Olson, Ron. 1992. "From Biola to the Barrio." Chapter 16 in *Coming Home: Why Protestant Clergy Are Becoming Orthodox*, ed. Peter Gillquist. Ben Lomand, Calif.: Conciliar Press.

Olson, Ted. 2003. "Weblog: Some May Be Offended by Biola Exhibit on Reaching Culture." http://www.christianitytoday.com/ct/2003/107/13.0.html (accessed March 12, 2007).

O'Neill, Dan, ed. 1987. *The New Catholics: Contemporary Converts Tell Their Stories*. New York: Crossroad Publishing Company.

Oren, Emily. 2002. "A Place to Pray." *Again* 24, no. 1 (January–March): 28–30.

Pagitt, Doug. 2004. *Reimagining Spiritual Formation: A Week in the Life of an Experimental Church*. Grand Rapids, Mich.: Zondervan/Emergent/YS Books.

———. 2005a. *BodyPrayer: The Posture of Intimacy with God*. Colorado Springs, Colo.: Waterbrook Press.

———. 2005b. *Preaching Re-Imagined: The Role of the Sermon in Communities of Faith*. Grand Rapids, Mich.: Zondervan.

Pastore, Frank. 2004. "Christian Conservatives Must Not Compromise." *Los Angeles Times*, November 5, B 13.

Pearcy, Nancy. 2001. "Design and the Discriminating Public: Gaining a Hearing from Ordinary People." Chapter 2 in *Signs of Intelligence: Understanding Intelligent Design*, ed. William A. Dembski and James M. Kushiner. Grand Rapids, Mich.: Brazos Press.

Porterfield, Amanda. 2001. *The Transformation of American Religion: The Story of a Late Twentieth-Century Awakening*. New York: Oxford Univ. Press.

Postman, Neil. 1985. *Amusing Ourselves to Death: Public Discourse in the Age of Show Business*. New York: Penguin Books.

Prothero, Stephen. 2007. *Religious Literacy: What Every American Needs to Know—And Doesn't*. New York and San Francisco: HarperSanFrancisco.

Renfree, Fr. Thomas. 1992. "It Happened at Western Conservative Baptist." Chapter 5 in *Coming Home: Why Protestant Clergy Are Becoming Orthodox*, ed. Peter Gillquist. Ben Lomand, Calif.: Conciliar Press.

Riesebrodt, Martin. 1993. *Pious Passion: The Emergence of Modern Fundamentalism in the United States and Iran*. Berkeley: Univ. of California Press.

Roof, Wade Clark. 1993. *A Generation of Seekers: The Spiritual Journeys of the Baby Boom Generations*. New York: HarperCollins

———. 1999. *Spiritual Marketplace: Baby Boomers and the Remaking of American Religion*. Princeton, N.J.: Princeton Univ. Press.

Russinger, Greg, ed. 2005. *Practitioners: Voices within the Emerging Church* Ventura, Calif.: Regal.

Ryan, Marie-Laure. 2003. *Narrative as Virtual Reality: Immersion and Interactivity in Literature and Electronic Media*. Baltimore, Md.: Johns Hopkins Univ. Press.

Sargeant, Kimon Howland. 2000. *Seeker Churches: Promoting Traditional Religion in a Nontraditional Way.* New Brunswick, N.J.: Rutgers Univ. Press.

Schaeffer, Franky. 1981. *Addicted to Mediocrity: 20th Century Christians and the Arts.* Westchester, Ill: Crossway Books.

———. 1982. *A Time for Anger: The Myth of Neutrality.* Westchester, Ill: Crossway Books.

———. 1984. *Bad News for Modern Man: An Agenda for Christian Activism.* Westchester, Ill: Crossway Books.

Schaeffer, Frank. 2002 [1994]. *Dancing Alone.* Salisbury, Mass.: Regina Orthodox Press.

Schmidt, Leigh. 2005. *Restless Souls: The Making of American Spirituality.* San Francisco: HarperSanFrancisco.

Schuman, Howard, and Jacqueline Scott. 1989. "Generations and Collective Memories." *American Sociological Review* 54: 359–81.

Shanks, Niall. 2004. *God, the Devil, and Darwin: A Critique of Intelligent Design Theory.* New York: Oxford Univ. Press.

Shapiro, Ben. 2004. *Brainwashed: How Universities Indoctrinate America's Youth.* Nashville: Thomas Nelson.

Smith, Christian. 2003. *Moral Believing Animals: Human Personhood and Culture.* New York: Oxford Univ. Press.

Smith, Chuck, Jr. 2001. *The End of the World . . . As We Know It: Clear Direction for Bold and Innovative Ministry in a Postmodern World.* Colorado Springs, Colo.: Waterbrook Press.

Smith, James K. A. 2003. "The Economics of the Emerging Church." http://www.theooze.com/articles/print.cfm?id=654 (accessed November 16, 2005).

———. 2005. "A Little Story about Metanarratives: Lyotard, Religion, and Postmodernism Revisited." Chapter 5 in *Christianity and the Postmodern Turn: Six Views,* ed. Myron Penner. Grand Rapids, Mich.: Brazos Press.

Stanczak, Gregory C. 2006. *Engaged Spirituality: Social Change and American Religion.* New Brunswick, N.J., and London: Rutgers Univ. Press.

Strauss, William, and Neil Howe. 1991. *Generations: The History of America's Future, 1584 to 2069.* New York: Quill/William Morrow.

Stephens, Mitchell. 1998. *The Rise of the Image, the Fall of the Word.* New York: Oxford Univ. Press.

Sweet, Leonard. 1999a. *AquaChurch: Essential Leadership Arts for Piloting Your Church in Today's Fluid Culture.* Loveland, Colo.: Group Publishing.

———. 1999b. *SoulTsunami: Sink or Swim in the New Millennium Culture.* Grand Rapids, Mich.: Zondervan.

————. 2000a. *Post-Modern Pilgrims: First Century Passion for the 21st Century World*. Nashville: Broadman and Holman Publishers.

————. 2000b. *Soul Salsa: 17 Surprising Steps for Godly Living in the 21st Century*. Grand Rapids, Mich.: Zondervan.

————. 2001. *Carpe Mañana: Is Your Church Ready to Seize Tomorrow?* Grand Rapids, Mich.: Zondervan.

Sweet, Leonard, ed. 2003. *The Church in Emerging Culture: Five Perspectives*. Grand Rapids, Mich.: Zondervan/Emergent/YS Books.

Tapscott, Don. 1998. *Growing Up Digital: The Rise of the Net Generation*. New York: McGraw-Hill.

Taylor, Justin. 2004. "Introduction: Postconservative Evangelicalism and the Rest of This Book." In *Reclaiming the Center: Confronting Evangelical Accommodation in Postmodern Times*, ed. Millard J. Erickson, Paul Kjoss Helseth, and Justin Taylor. Wheaton, Ill: Crossway Books.

Taylor, Steve. 2005. *The Out of Bounds Church? Learning to Create a Community of Faith in a Culture of Change*. Grand Rapids, Mich.: Zondervan/Emergent/YS Books.

Trammel, Madison. 2007. "Striking Out the Liberals." *Christianity Today*, January 26, 2007. http://www.christianitytoday.com/ct/2007/february/20.31.html (accessed January 28, 2007).

Trueheart, Charles. 1996. "Welcome to the Next Church," *The Atlantic Monthly* 278, no. 2 (August): 37–58.

Twitchell, James B. 2004. *Branded Nation: The Marketing of Megachurch, College Inc., and Museumworld*. New York: Simon and Schuster.

Veith, Gene Edward. 2003. *Loving God with All Your Mind: Thinking as a Christian in the Postmodern World*, rev. ed. Wheaton, Ill: Crossway Books.

Verran, Helen. 2001. *Science and an African Logic*. Chicago: Univ. of Chicago Press.

Wallis, Jim. 2005a. *Faith Works: How to Live Your Beliefs and Ignite Positive Social Change*. New York: Random House.

————. 2005b. *God's Politics: Why the Right Gets It Wrong and the Left Doesn't Get It*. San Francisco: HarperSanFrancisco.

Warren, Rick. 2002. *The Purpose-Driven Life*. Grand Rapids, Mich.: Zondervan.

Watson, Walter. 1985. *The Architectonics of Meaning: Foundations of the New Pluralism*. Albany: State Univ. of New York Press.

Webber, Robert E. 1985. *Evangelicals on the Canterbury Trail: Why Evangelicals Are Attracted to the Liturgical Church*. Harrisburg, Pa.: Morehouse Publishing.

————. 1999. *Ancient-Future Faith: Rethinking Evangelicalism for a Postmodern World*. Grand Rapids, Mich.: Baker Books.

————. 2002. *The Younger Evangelicals: Facing the Challenges of the New World*. Grand Rapids, Mich.: Baker Books.

Weber, Max. 1993 [1963]. *The Sociology of Religion*. Boston: Beacon Press.

———. 2002 [1930]. *The Protestant Ethic and the Spirit of Capitalism*. London: Routledge.

West, John G., Jr. 2001. "The Regeneration of Science and Culture: The Cultural Implications of Scientific Materialism Versus Intelligent Design." Chapter 4 in *Signs of Intelligence: Understanding Intelligent Design*, ed. William A. Dembski and James M. Kushiner. Grand Rapids, Mich.: Brazos Press.

Wilkerson, David. 1966. *The Cross and the Switchblade*. Grand Rapids, Mich.: Fleming H. Revell.

Willard, Dallas. 1988. *The Spirit of the Disciplines: Understanding How God Changes Lives*. San Francisco: HarperSanFrancisco.

Winston, Diane. 2004. "Framing Power." February 4, 2004. http://www.therevealer.org/archives/feature_000180.php (accessed April 1, 2005).

Wright, N. T. 1997. *What Saint Paul Really Said: Was Paul of Tarsus the Real Founder of Christianity?* Grand Rapids, Mich.: Eerdmans.

———. 2000. *The Challenge of Jesus: Rediscovering Who Jesus Was and Is*. London: SPCK.

Wuthnow, Robert. 1994. *I Come Away Stronger: How Small Groups Are Changing American Religion*. Grand Rapids, Mich.: Eerdmans.

———. 1998. *After Heaven: Spirituality in America Since the 1950s*. Berkeley and Los Angeles: Univ. of California Press

——— 2001. *Creative Spirituality: The Way of the Artist*. Berkeley and Los Angeles: Univ. of California Press.

———. 2003. *All in Sync: How Music and Art are Revitalizing American Religion*. Berkeley and Los Angeles: Univ. of California Press.

Young, Matt, and Taner Edis. 2004. *Why Intelligent Design Fails: A Scientific Critique of the New Creationism*. New Brunswick, N.J.: Rutgers Univ. Press.

INDEX

Italicized page numbers refer to illustrations.

ABOUT THE AUTHORS

RICHARD FLORY is a research associate in the Center for Religion and Civic Culture at the University of Southern California. His Ph.D. is in sociology, from the University of Chicago. He is the editor of *GenX Religion* (Routledge, 2000), and has written several articles and book chapters on different aspects of religion in America. He has also created three interactive, multimedia art gallery installations: with Donald Miller and Daniel Callis, "Finding Faith: Christianity in a New Generation" (2003) and "Christianity and Culture: Four Emerging Forms" (2003 and 2004); and with Daniel Callis, "The Postmodern Metropolis: Los Angeles, Tijuana and Las Vegas" (2004). He is currently working on a book examining the different life experiences of African American, Asian, Hispanic, and white teenagers. His research has been supported by grants from the Louisville Institute, the Pew Charitable Trusts, the Lilly Endowment, and the University of Southern California.

DONALD E. MILLER is the Firestone Professor of Religion at the University of Southern California. He serves as executive director of the Center for Religion and Civic Culture and as director of the School of Religion. He received the Ph.D. degree in religion (social ethics) from USC in 1975. He is the author, coauthor, or editor of eight books, including *Global Pentecostalism: The New Face of Christian Social Engagement* (University of California Press, 2007), *Armenia: Portraits of Survival and Hope* (University of California Press, 2003), *GenX Religion* (Routledge,

2000), *Reinventing American Protestantism* (University of California Press, 1997), *Survivors: An Oral History of the Armenian Genocide* (University of California Press, 1993), *Homeless Families: The Struggle for Dignity* (University of Illinois Press, 1993), *Writing and Research in Religious Studies* (Prentice Hall, 1992), and *The Case for Liberal Christianity* (Harper and Row, 1981). The emerging focus of his research is on international faith-based NGOs, and involves work in Rwanda, Tanzania, and Armenia. He has had major grants from the Lilly Endowment, the John Templeton Foundation, the Pew Charitable Trusts, the Ford Foundation, the Irvine Foundation, the Haynes Foundation, the California Council for the Humanities, and the Fieldstead Company.